If Grandma's in Heaven, Watch Out!

The 1930's Bonrud Gang

by

Ken Halverson

Bloomington, IN   Milton Keynes, UK

authorHOUSE®

AuthorHouse™
1663 Liberty Drive, Suite 200
Bloomington, IN 47403
www.authorhouse.com
Phone: 1-800-839-8640

AuthorHouse™ UK Ltd.
500 Avebury Boulevard
Central Milton Keynes, MK9 2BE
www.authorhouse.co.uk
Phone: 08001974150

*This book is a work of non-fiction. Unless otherwise noted, the author
and the publisher make no explicit guarantees as to the accuracy of*

First published by AuthorHouse 4/19/2007

ISBN: 978-1-4343-0517-6 (sc)

Printed in the United States of America
Bloomington, Indiana

This book is printed on acid-free paper.

Contents

FOREWORD

This is a true story that takes place during the 1920's and 1930's. It's about the dangerous 7 member Bonrud Gang from Minnesota. It's about my grandparents and great uncles.

This story takes you back to World War I before the Bonrud Gang was formed with a brief explanation how the Doughboys as a whole went through pains surviving the WW I, Liquor Prohibition, Roaring 20's and the most hurtful the Great Economic Depression during the 1930's also known as The Great Stock Market Crash.

Some people say that because of the above factors many people made the choice to form gangs for the purpose of creating a criminal kingdom. There have been statements made, "people had to do what ever was necessary to survive". This is a poor excuse for turning to crime for the sole purpose of advancing ones self at the expense of hurting others. Fortunately they were a minority of the population and all things being equal; the majority of the population did not turn to crime. The majority went through the tough times working hard for their worldly possessions.

Today there are a few that just want to forget the gangsters and the wrongs they committed and avoid this era all together. They want everyone, "To forgive them. It all happened long ago." These people just don't want to deal with facts. The truth of matter is gangs and there activities seriously hurt people. Not only extortion and robberies were committed against innocent people, some people died as a direct result of criminal activity. If you are a relative, friend, or sympathizer of the gangsters it's really not your place to say, "Forgive them, it's in the past". Or say, "It's in the past, get over it". This is for the victims to say. They have that right to forgive and forget, not you. I'm sure there are some people are going to ask, "Why did he drag this old hateful period out in the open now?"

If a story of this magnitude is buried in history how can we understand and deal with our present day gang behavior? The gangs back then and today are not Robin Hood and his Merry Men. They are ruthless gun wielding robbers and killers. They steal from everybody and keep what they take.

Did any gang improve the way of life for the majority? Did the gangs have any positive impact of bringing the country out of the Depression? How about contributing a solution to avoid a world war? Did they improve the life style of the American public? I have researched their activities and found they didn't contribute anything to society other than job security for law enforcement personnel.

To those people that excuse the formation of gangs because of a series of unfortunate country wide events during the 1920's and 1930's -- stop it and get real. Chances are these gangsters would have formed their criminal activity no matter what shape the "State of the Union" was in

This is a true story. This is a story of a gang that hurt people during their time period and how they affected a family through out their lives. This gang was so prolific in their criminal behavior the authorities had to change the way they treated criminals that took the Twin Cities as a safe haven taking refuge from out state law authorities.

This is a story about my grandparents and great uncles that formed a gang for the sole purpose of enriching themselves at the cost of the innocent. I make no excuses for their behavior and I tell it the way it happened. If they were formed today I would consider them armed and extremely dangerous.

GANGS

Before I can tell you about the Bonrud Gang we need to understand the historical time period when they began in earnest to form a 1930's type gang. Make no mistake about gangs; they have been in the USA for a long time. It was a gang that dumped the tea into the Boston Harbor in 1773. New York City had some of the most vicious gangs during the early to mid 1800's. That's farther back than we need to go. Let's talk about the modern gangs, the ones we recognize.

Gangs back in the 1920's and 1930's were sometimes thought to be like Robin Hood and his Merry Men who preyed on the rich and gave to the poor. What were you thinking? These gangs back then were ruthless killers, thieves and con artists. Their armed robberies at the time were against anybody, rich or poor. Their booty certainty did not get to the poor. They kept it!

I like to consider in simple terms the gangs different styles and operations and then compare them to each other as they went through the decades.

The individual gangster during the 1920's – 1930's carried a personal weapon of choice. Usually it would be a .32 or .38 caliber revolver hand gun. They are light and easy to conceal. Those gangsters that couldn't afford a hand gun were reduced to using a knife, club or just threats.

The use of threats with or without the use of a weapon is known as a "strong armed hold up". The use of physical threats could backfire on the bad guy if the intended victim resisted. A fist fight could result with the bad guy losing and possibly being arrested and tossed in jail or in a hospital. Physical hand to hand violence was a desperate move.

Another and more frequent crime in that era was to kidnap a person, steal their valuables, including a car, and hold the victim for ransom. Keep in mind while these crimes were going on it was during the Great Depression. The kidnappers didn't hold out a lot of hope for ransom. People were broke back then. More often than not the car and personal effects would satisfy the gang. It was enough to pawn off for a few dollars and then purchase some liquor, beer or groceries.

The big time gangs that drew attention to themselves could be classified into 3 different groups. You may agree or disagree. It certainly isn't any kind of official opinion. From what I studied over the years this is my personal observation.

GANGS THAT OPERATE FOR A PROFIT

Gangs that formed in major cities like Chicago, New York, and Miami would be a service oriented gang. I mean this in worse possible forum. Al Capone is always a good example. He had Capitalist ideas; supply, demand and profit. There was a demand for hard liquor, beer, prostitution, and a safe place to part take in these activities, a "Speak Easy" or in real words, a saloon.

A Speak Easy was a place within the gangster's downtown territory. As pictured in such television shows like "The Untouchables", the

Speak Easy was an exclusive place for a gangster screened citizen to enjoy the entertainment supplied by the gang. Entering the Speak Easy was an adventure of its own. The place would be in a secluded downtown location. The people would have a secret way of knocking at the door for admission. On the other side of the door there stood a guard to protect entry. He would open a tiny peep hole in the door. If he recognized the person knocking, he would allow entry. Sometimes a password would be needed. If the guard did not recognize the person and the person was extremely persistent in entering, then the guard could assume it is a raid by authorities. He would sound the alarm and all the people inside would be led out of the Speak Easy through secret doors and tunnels and dissipate into the night.

If all things went according to the gangs plan, the beat cop patrolling the area around the Speak Easy would have advance notice of an impending raid. The beat cop would be on the gangs' payroll and for his pay he would warn the gang of a raid. That night when the authorities raided the Speak Easy, the building would be empty.

Capone's gang would protect their self proclaimed territory with bullets. To keep his illegal operation running he would pay off the police, city officials and some judges. On the other hand, if other gangs tried to infiltrate his territory, serious retaliation would be swift and deadly. The gangs of that era executed each others men with very public drive by shootings and bombings. These gangs usually kept the violence between themselves and very seldom imposed violence against the public. After all, it was the public they focused on as customers.

Extortion was another means of income used by gangs of this era. Gangs would approach a business owner and offer them protection from robberies for a price. The ones offering protection are the ones committing the robberies. If the business man refused the offer, they could expect an escalating degree of violence against him until either his business is blown up and destroyed by the gang, or the owner and his family would face grave bodily harm or death. One way or another, the gang would win and receive the payments.

SPREE KILLERS

Gangs that roamed from state to state were the most dangerous of all. I would be hard pressed to call them gangs as much as I would call them spree killers. The likes of Dillenger, Machine Gun Kelly and Baby Face Nelson were loners that became cold blooded killers. Pairs and groups that would be good examples would be Bonnie and Clyde and the Ma Barker gang. These people were roamers. They would travel from state to state holding up banks, stores and individuals for any amount of money they could get. What separates them is their violent temper. Innocent people and lawmen alike would be gunned down for no apparent reason. When individuals were gunned down it would have been spawned from a hold up gone wrong, resisting their demands, or being collateral damage during a shoot out. These were the most desperate of all gangs. The relentless pursuit by lawmen made these gangsters edgy and very short tempered. Very seldom could these people sleep with both eyes closed. They just never knew when a lawman would appear before them.

REGIONAL HOLD UP GANGS

This is the group that traveled from city to city acting more like the "gangs that couldn't shoot straight". They were unpredictable in their crimes very random. Usually they were localized in a city and committed their crimes within a certain radius of their home base. The Bonrud gang is the best example I can use. They threatened violence but seldom enforced it beyond physical violence. They imposed their authority in numbers of members and weapons.

Kidnapping and car jacking was their favored method of crime. Small town gas stations and grocery stores became the victims. This type gang would be organized and close to each other. If anyone ever did get shot while being victimized, it was more by accident than design.

Organized crime that began in the 1920's was a direct result of Mafia proliferation. Now don't get me wrong on this topic, I'm not a professional analyst when it comes to explaining Mafia behavior, but there are a few things I have learned over the years.

THE MAFIA

The Mafia was also present during the early 1920's. I would say it was in its infancy. The 1920's -1930's gangs erupted from the infant Mafia. The gangs back then had bosses that were spawned from Mafia leaders who brought themselves to the U.S.A., the land of opportunity, from over seas. The Mafia power just started to bloom in the early 1930's.

During the 1940's it grew silently and then during the 1950's it began to have a strangle hold on large unions, large labor forces, ship yards, airports, and the beginning of illegal drug distribution. Using stolen money from pension funds also allowed them to start their style of gambling in Los Vegas. Their growth snowballed into a major illegal power by the 1980's.

The Mafia was a quiet operation. Each major city had a Mafia family. Some cities had more than one family. New York City and Chicago had several Mafia families. They each acted like a corporation with their families extending operations nation wide. Some families got along with each other very well, so well in fact, they would conduct periodic meetings with the Godfathers of each family. Operations, profits and losses would be discussed. If one family had a beef with another, it was in this forum that they would present each others case before the rest of the Godfathers. Hopefully they would all come to a peaceful solution. If a solution couldn't be agreed to, a war between the two gangs would be sanctioned by the rest of the Godfathers. The sanctioned war would only involve the two opposing families with the others staying out of it.

After a war was started and high profile killings were being exposed in the newspapers, the rest of the families would step in and regain control of the situation. Public exposure was the last thing any Mafia boss wanted.

To bring a rogue Godfather under control would sometimes involve a sanctioned contract for murder. Once the Godfather was dead, the rest of the family would fall into the ranks of the remaining families or a new Godfather would be sanctioned and appointed.

Quietly infiltrating into large unions like the Teamsters and Dockworkers allowed them to steal millions of dollars from trust funds and pension funds. It also gave them insight to expensive shipments of goods and cash as it was trucked across the country or unloaded from a ship. They had spies everywhere searching for a large bounty to steal. Extortion was common place against small business. The Mafia always wanted to offer protection for a piece of the income. This was a great source of income for a family.

They committed their executions on a business level. Murder was generally authorized by a Godfather. It was carried out as a contract between the Godfather and a hit man of his choice. The murder, or execution, was conducted swift and without witness. The body would be disposed in a way where it would never be discovered. If a body was ever discovered it was by design and its discovery served as a warning to other Mafia gangs that the deceased committed a violation of Mafia trust and this serves notice that violating this trust is deadly. The Mafia moved under cover and with very little exposure.

It was Gotti that changed every thing that previous Godfathers held close; the Mafia bosses always wanted to operate with a low profile and quietly in the corners of crime.

Gotti took over his very major family with a very public execution of his boss by having his assassins shoot him to death in front of a down town steak house where crowds roamed the sidewalks. The ego driven Gotti even conducted his gangster meetings in the open by roaming the sidewalk in front of his hangout conducting business with his under bosses. He was brazen enough to conduct neighborhood block parties complete with fireworks. He performed these exhibitions to gain public support.

Gotti always dressed in extremely expensive suites. He was a striking looking man when dressed up. Magazines and newspapers enjoyed having his picture and a brief story about him in their articles. His image sold magazines. Don't let his good looks fool you. This man was a very prolific mobster that grew through the Mafia ranks by committing extreme violence including brutal murders. He was the muscle of a Mafia Family for many years before he rose through the ranks to become a Godfather by murder.

Other Godfathers were in disgust with his over exposure. These very dramatic actions drew public attention to him and the Mafia. It also drew the federal authority's attention. As a result of some of this over exposure the FBI was able to gather evidence through electronic and hands on surveillance. This allowed a series arrests and trials. He was put on trial a couple different times with felony charges and was found innocent every time. He was tagged the Teflon Don. Criminal charges against him never stuck.

He eventually opened his mouth to wide one day and made threats against his number one man Jimmy the Bull. These conversations were secretly recorded by the F.B.I. and played to The Bull. This terrified the Bull and he was afraid that Gotti was going to assassinate him.

The Bull decided to become a turn coat and tell federal authorities everything about the Gotti family business. For this information the Bull received protection under the Federal Witness Protection Program and a small prison sentence. The Teflon wore off with Gotti's final trial. He was charged and found guilty of several RICO (Racketeer Influenced and Corrupt Organization act) crimes and sentenced to life in prison. He died in prison at the age of 61 on June 10, 2002 from neck cancer. The Mafia has been somewhat quiet ever since his death.

The Gangs Of Today

Setting aside organized gangs like the Hells Angels, a very well organized motorcycle gang operating nationwide, radical anti government gangs, K.K.K. and their subsidiaries, and what's left of the Mafia, or the Costa Nostra, what can anyone say about the gangs of today? For the most part I believe they are disorganized juvenile delinquents. They are the result of the neighborhood gangs that formed during the late 1950's. The gangs back then weren't nearly as deadly as the gangs of today. Back in the 1950's disputes were handled by so called "rumbles". Fist fights with clubs and brass knuckles, and the gangs all standing toe to toe with each other in an alley fighting with each other until there was a clear winner. There was no cowardly ambushing back then. Guns? They didn't need them. They handled things with their fist. Very seldom was anyone killed. If a person was killed during a rumble, it was a total accident.

Today's gangs are influenced by a few leaders that promise teenage boys and girls adventure beyond their dreams. It's usually drugs that give them the dreams. These little gangsters are short tempered little thugs that somehow, through illegal means, get a weapon and impose their misguided power unto others. They are shooting each other for as little as a head bandana, t-shirt or jacket. They proclaim they own certain colors and hand signs and they hold them in high esteem. They are territorial and very protective of the boundaries. If any outsider use their colors, hand signals, or cross the boundary, it would most certainly be death to that person. These kids have no fear of dying for their own gang and many do. On the other hand they also have no hesitation in committing murder. These gangs are dangerous to the public. These are misguided and under developed youngsters. I believe they are from a depressed family with very little guidance and supervision. They posses misguided beliefs of a better life through a gang. They adopt the gang as a family that grants them freedoms that are in reality illegal activities. Selling drugs, strong arm robberies, robbing various stores and home invasions are their sources of income. Public collateral damage is high when these gangs are on the prowl for a victim. Random wild shootings and misidentification is the terror they impose on innocent people. Many innocent people are murdered in this fashion. It's been asked by many officials why do these gangs exists? The parents, guardians and gang members always have the same excuse. The kids have nothing else to do. That is the biggest load of bull for an excuse they could ever use. What's wrong with school? What's wrong with joining the military? How about getting a job? That's the same type of excuse that was used during the 1930's. Depression drove the gangster to the life of crime. It's always somebody else's fault. Parent and guardians live in denial. When a little brat is caught and the parent is notified, their response is usually, "My little boy couldn't possibly be a gangster. He's a good boy."

Wake up people! Own up to your responsibility raising your children. Don't let a prison guard raise them.

Going back to the 1930's the likes of Al Capone, Bugs Moran, Bonnie and Clyde, and Ma Barker kept the police quite busy. Large cities such as New York City, Miami, and Chicago were infested with gangs fighting each other for territory rights. For relief from the fighting and bickering, the gangsters would take refuge in St. Paul and Minneapolis. The Twin Cities were known to the gangsters as a place of refuge and comfort without police running them out of town. It was in Minnesota the gangs could get a good night's rest and some entertainment before embarking on another crime spree. Minneapolis and St. Paul was John Dillenger's favorite refuge. He admitted that he felt safe there.

In Minnesota, the Bonrud Gang, a Regional Hold up Gang, worked their criminal activities quietly and under the police radar. This gang roamed Minneapolis in search of a victim for a car jacking. Once a victim was located, the car jacking was swift and completed in seconds with the victim driving under the direction of a gun wielding gangster. When they were eventually caught, they admitted to committing over 63 kidnappings and armed hold ups throughout Minnesota and Iowa.

It was the lack of technology that kept them so prolific. Most country police cars were not equipped with radios and most roadside gas stations didn't have telephones. They were lucky if they had gas or electric utilities. The Depression didn't leave them enough money to have luxury items like telephones anyway.

The gang operated for a few years without being noticed. It all caught up to them eventually in a little town in western Minnesota called Benson. What happened there hasn't been equaled since.

In 1994 I made a trip to Benson. I couldn't believe my ears. There were people still living there that remembered the shootout and trial.

This was so interesting. I had a chance to meet with the local police chief from Benson and Montevideo. They weren't around at the time, but they listened to many stories from their predecessors and elders about how these small town lawmen, short in number but long in ability, captured them and how the legal system tried these desperadoes under stressful conditions.

The gang members were in part, Duco and Mabel, my grandparents. Cleon and Nobel are my great uncles. As the story goes on you will discover the other three members. Up until the time of their deaths, they thought that their criminal activities were forgotten with time from the younger generations. I'm sure my grandparents were certain of this. Writing this book about them just goes to show you, criminals are stupid no matter what category or era they fall in.

HOW IT STARTED

Prior to 1929, our country was celebrating the end to WWI (1914-1918) with what we thought was a fairly strong economy. The Doughboys were home and ready for love, work, and play. This was the war to end all wars and the boys that fought and supported it were tired and wanted a way to vent.

We refer to these times as the Roaring 20's, but the boys had to party fast. There was a political movement going on that was about to ban the sale of intoxicating beverages. This movement was gaining speed and endorsement by political leaders. The 1920's party rolled on and we were dancing in the street and carrying the party on until the wee hours of 1929. The only intoxicating beverage available was purchased illegally. Then it happened. The stock market took a nosedive.

The "Crash of 1929" was an ugly period for these United States. This was the worse possible news that could hit this country since the war. It literally brought this country to its knees. We were frozen in an economic time warp. Wall Street was in turmoil. Money and stocks were losing value fast. Millionaires were becoming penniless. The ripple effect went all the way down to the youngster that had pennies in a savings account in a bank. Those who relied on trading in the stock market for a living were being asked to pay for their credits. Some of these credits were worth millions of dollars. These people had no cash to pay these debts and it contributed to more problems for Wall Street. The pressure on these investors to pay up caused so much personal depression that suicide was nearly the rule rather than the exception.

Large and small businesses were failing in record numbers with no replacements foreseen in the future. Banks were hemorrhaging money. Those who held bonds and bank certificates now help scrap paper. Those papers were worthless. Even the smallest savings accounts were drained by the banks in order to pay some of their debt but the banks still ran out of money and closed. Between 1929 and 1932, over 11,000 banks closed their doors.

Housing mortgages weren't being met and foreclosures were at an all-time high. Now the banks owned property that was worthless. People didn't have the capital to buy a foreclosed home at a drastically reduced price. Money was gone. The best of times turned into the worst of times, almost overnight.

Hobos! Bums! That is what the few people with money called the men on the street begging for nickels and dimes. Far from being hobos and bums, these men would perform any kind of labor for any kind of wage. At one time these men who had loving families, roofs over their heads, food on their tables, and decent jobs were reduced to begging and eating in food kitchens. These same men who'd seen the horrors of war and fought a war to end all wars now were fighting a different war, an economic war. This war had many more casualties on all fronts.

I can't imagine how humiliating that was on those poor souls. I heard stories of children finding ketchup bottles and bringing them home. They would rinse them out with water and have a "tomato" soup of sorts. For most, a cardboard shack was constructed for shelter. One thing that could have made this whole ordeal somewhat bearable would have been a bit of alcohol to sooth the nerves. That wasn't going to happen because of Carrie Nation, (November 25, 1846-June 9, 1911), an ax wielding anti-liquor activist, helped in the activation of the Eighteenth Amendment to the Constitution, also known as the Volstead Act. It banned the sale of intoxicating beverages. It was introduced and passed December 18, 1917, ratified January 16, 1919, and enforced as law January 16, 1920.

Thirty-six states went for this amendment. It was repealed December 5, 1933. The point being is that citizens had to go through this major Depression sober.

Why would there be such a movement like this in the first place? Were our lawmakers mad? As it turns out, when the Dough Boys came home from serving our country during WW1, alcohol was the choice for depressing the horrors of war for the solders that were in the European conflict. I can't imagine the fear a person could experience fighting not only for your country, but fighting for your own life. For days and months these brave men would be in a trench with bullets flying over their heads, bombs and artillery shells exploding all around them, mustard gas poisoning them into permanent disability or death. Phosphorous bombs exploding and sending this chemical into the body and burning to a person to death from the inside out. How terrifying was it to see the person next to you have a limb blown off by a bomb, or shot dead, or worse, shot in place where it was extremely painful and there is nothing you can do to help while he lay there screaming. Can you imagine fighting for your life against a foe that is doing the same thing? Try and imagine fighting hand to hand or with bayonet's, knives, bare fist, or a rock to bash a head in. The horror of war haunts a person for life.

The soldiers that tried to forget the horrors of war through alcohol eventually became serious and some times dangerous alcoholics. We didn't treat the cause back then. Today we recognize Post Traumatic Stress Syndrome. Back then we didn't call it that, we called it "Shell Shock". This diagnosis even carried into the WW2 and the Korean Conflict. It wasn't until after the Viet Nam conflict did we finally give PTS a serious look and serious treatment. As far as Shell Shock went, there was no real effort to treat it. It was up to the individual to take care of themselves. After a serious rise in family disputes it was determined that alcohol was the cause. Stop the alcohol and it in turn will stop the violence. Our leaders just didn't get it back then. It was the wrong cure for the wrong disease and finally in 1933 it was realized.

We would eventually climb out of this Depression with the 1933 Presidential election. Franklin D Roosevelt (FDR) was elected. He didn't waste time expressing his opinions and then acting on recovering the economy. He didn't like what the banks were doing and he didn't like what big business was doing. One of the first things he did was to introduce the "New Deal" to the American public.

He was going to start huge government projects and build up our infrastructure. This would put millions back to work. An unpopular but necessary move he made was to close all the remaining banks for reorganization. He also created the FDIC protection you now use as insurance for your savings accounts. When the banks went through their mandated audit and could balance their books, the government would allow them to use the FDIC program. This would tell the banks future customers that should anything disastrous happen to their accounts; the government would protect their savings up to a certain amount.

He also held the large companies responsible for implementing unemployment insurance and health benefits. Those that complied were given first choices in participating in the government projects. There would be plenty of projects to pick from.

He also gave the people hope by conducting his famous "Fireside Chats" over the radio. These chats soothed our country's nerves more than anything. The newspaper articles of the time praised FDR for these chats. It was amazing just how much the Fireside Chats meant to the public. Even the people that had no home and wandered the street would stop by the nearest appliance store and listen to a radio. Some stores would put a radio outside so people could listen to their president. He had super star quality and status. He would tell the American citizens that the president was optimistic about our future and he was truly on the side of the people. The people took notice. The public simply adored him.

People still wanted liquor, and there were those who would supply it. It didn't matter how poor a person was, they always seemed have just enough cash to buy that shot of liquor.

A few things vulcanized themselves together and turned into the largest multiplex business of all: distilling liquor, brewing beer, gambling, Speak Easies (saloons), and prostitution. The two things that made these things so profitable were unemployment and the Volstead Act.

These things were the launching pad for many gangsters of the time. Of course, the biggest name in gangsters was Al Capone, whose town was Chicago. He eventually became one of the richest men in the country. His wealth was once estimated at over 11 million dollars.

What a business this fellow Capone had. He bootlegged (hijacked the trucks) liquor from Canada, watered it down, and served it in his saloons at an inflated price. He had his own beer breweries scattered all over the countryside and of course; he had a prostitution ring that complemented all his other activities. His gambling operations were slanted in his favor. His customers didn't care what the prices were, or if the cocktails were watered down. They cared less if his prostitutes had disease, or even if he cheated at gambling. They came to the Speak Easies to have fun, and fun they found. All these activities were illegal but that made it exciting. One never knew when the time was up for any particular Speak Easy. A police raid could be just around the comer. Funny thing, though. Capone very rarely had raids on his Speak Easies. Very few of his beer breweries were broken up by authorities, and his hijackings went un-investigated. How was this possible?

Local city officials were paid off every week. Capone had everyone in his pocket. Local police and the upper police echelon, city council members, the city manager was being paid off, and several judges. If it was someone that could hurt him, he would pay them off. It should also be mentioned that his generosity only went so far. If a person tried to squeeze too much out of Capone, it would be a bullet in the head and a lesson to the rest. He was generous, but ruthless. It was just business to Capone. Payola, as it was called, was a common thing back then-- if they had a new cop on the beat, they would give him a bit of payola to turn his back on things that he shouldn't see.

There were people that wouldn't take his money. They would rather take his business and his life.

O'Bannon and Moran were his competitors and nemeses. Chicago was a huge city at the time, but not to these three. These gangsters would fight for buildings. The more buildings they won would eventually mean control of a city block. The three of them went around and around killing each other's men in gang wars. Kids today that think they have gang wars, ha—they're just small time punks compared to what these three men did to each other.

Day after day the shootouts would happen, day and night. The morgue had never been so busy. They couldn't bury them fast enough. These gangs thrived on these battles. It was almost a mandatory procedure. I hit your headquarters one day, and you retaliated by hitting mine the next.

One such shooting occurred during the day. It happened while Capone was at his favorite restaurant. A car drove by slow when all of a sudden from the car blasted the sound of a Chicago Typewriter. That was what the gangs called Thompson submachine guns. Capone was standing outside at the time when the guns were aimed at the restaurant. With a stunned look on his face, he looked around and noticed there were no bullet holes anywhere. "They're shooting blanks!" he yelled at his bodyguards.

About the same time the words came out of his mouth the bodyguards tackled him and pulled him into the restaurant. At that exact time three more cars drove by and started shooting. Capone laughed at them and was beginning to stand up and fire back at them when all of a sudden bullets started hitting everything around him. Once again the bodyguards pulled him down. The first car was a decoy. It was also supposed to inspire confidence in Capone and draw him out into the open. Capone's bodyguards were smarter than that. They figured it out.

Finally Capone had enough of the back and forth shootings. Some of them were getting a little too close. He was going to end this bickering once and for all. Capone set up an ambush on Moran. He planned the February 14, 1933 Valentine's Day massacre. Several of

Moran's men were lured into a warehouse under the impression they were going to receive a truckload of liquor. Moran was supposed to be there but he was running late.

Seven of Moran's men entered the warehouse. Just a few seconds later, Capone's men dressed in police uniforms entered the building. As they entered, they were shouting orders for the seven men to line up against the wall. These men thought that these were zealous cops trying to impress them and eventually negotiate some protection money from them.

Not the case. When the seven were lined up against the wall, several other Capone's men entered the building and pulled out machineguns from under their coats and opened fire on those helpless seven men. Over 1000 rounds were fired. Some of the bodies were completely tom apart. There was a blood pool over forty feet in diameter. This was the cruelest shooting of all.

Capone was questioned but he had a great alibi. He was at his Florida retreat when all this happened. He got away with murder. Not a shock. He'd been getting away with murder for years.

The Federal Government took notice of the massacre. The Valentine's Day shooting made national news. The pressure was on the FBI from the general public and Washington DC politicians. The FBI finally decided to step in and save the fine citizens of Chicago. J. Edgar Hoover, head of the FBI, brought Elliot Ness into the weave. His orders were to shut down Capone. Whatever it took shut him down. He had become a burden and embarrassment and Hoover could no longer bear it. His reputation as being the top lawman in the country was at stake.

Ness took the case and proceeded to root out the criminal element from Chicago. Some may remember a television program "The Untouchables" starring Robert Stack. It was about the successes

Elliot Ness had in Chicago busting breweries and arresting the bad guys every week. That was the television version of Elliot Ness.

Actually, Ness soon figured out that Capone was smarter than he gave him credit for. At every juncture along the way, Ness was being foiled. When he thought he had a good lead on a brewery, he would gather the troops and bust the place. When he and his men went storming into the building, it was already converted into a sewing factory. This was Ness's luck for a couple of years. Occasionally he would get lucky and find a brewery. He would destroy it one day and it would be rebuilt the next day. The same went for the Speak Easies, raid one day and they would be open the next day. If he arrested anyone, the paid off judge would fine the bad guy and set him free. Of course, the fines were paid by the gang's boss. If by chance a jail sentence couldn't be avoided, the convicted would spend his time in luxury.

It finally took a bookkeeper to put Capone in prison. The bookkeeper inventoried Capone's revenue and found that Capone didn't pay his fair share of taxes. This was a big time Federal offense. Not quite what they wanted to bust him for, but it was a conviction. It would take him out of action.

Capone was convicted in October 1931 and sent to prison for eleven years. Some of his time was served at Alcatraz; the toughest prison of all. He also had to pay an $80,000.00 fine. That was pocket money for him. Capone did his time and by all accounts he was a model prisoner. He was released in 1939 suffering from advanced syphilis. He lived out his life getting closer to complete insanity. He died in Florida in 1947 a babbling idiot.

Back then it was Capone, Capone, and more Capone. He put himself on the pedestal. It's got to be remembered that there were other gangsters around back then that were even more dangerous.

These men killed because they liked it. Not for money, but for fun; Dillenger, Bonnie and Clyde, Dutch Shultz, Baby Face Nelson, Pretty Boy Floyd, (Bugsie) Ben Seagal, Vito Genovese, and Charles (Lucky) Luciano. These guys were monsters and cold-blooded killers.

These were the names that appeared in the newspapers on a daily basis. Not all gangsters could bootleg, run a brothel, or run a saloon. You would think robbing banks would net some cash. Not so. FDR closed the banks and the ones that reopened were short on cash. Gas stations and grocery stores carried more cash. The country was put on rations for food and fuel. It can almost be compared to our problems in the late 1970's and earlier 2000's when we had shortages of gas. Those days weren't near as bad as the 1920's shortages. Kidnapping became the real moneymaker of the day for the bad guys. It was becoming epidemic. Every day in nearly every city a kidnapping occurred.

It was the American hero Charles Lindbergh's son who was kidnapped and made national attention. Lindbergh was the aviator that was the first to fly across the Atlantic Ocean in 33 hours. He made instant celebrity status.

In the middle of the night a person put up a ladder to his son's window, climbed it, snatched the baby boy, and got away. Later a $50,000.00 ransom was paid. In return, a dead body was retrieved. Investigations lead police to arrest Bruno Hauptman. He was tried in a court of law, convicted, and sentenced to death. He was executed a short time later. It has been brought to the nation's attention that he may not have committed the crime. Evidence shown to the public on various TV programs brings up reasonable doubt. Could we have executed an innocent man? That's another story.

Minnesota wasn't to be left out of this nationwide crime spree. Unknown to Minnesota law enforcement, the Bonrud gang was formed in the early days of 1932. Its members were Cleon and Margaret Bonrud, Nobel and Blanch Bonrud, Perley (aka Duke, Duco) Oliva, Mabel (aka Bonrud, Peterson), Oliva and Walter Christenson, a close friend to Cleon. Cleon, Nobel, and Mabel were brothers and sister. Walter and Cleon met in the St. Cloud Reformatory and became quick friends. Walter was serving time for armed robbery and Cleon, for grand larceny. Their respective crime sprees started in the late 1920's. Nobel had a long police record but he was able to avoid prison time. Prior to 1932, Mabel, Blanch, and Margaret had no official police record. Duco had a liquor violation conviction.

Everyone in the gang lived in Minneapolis. They were all transplanted from western and southwestern Minnesota. Most of the gang was from the Swift County and the Chippewa County area.

Cleon and Walter were the sparks that ignited the Bonrud Gang. When they were released from prison, they went on a crime spree of armed robberies in southern Minnesota and northern Iowa.

When the area got too hot for them, they would retreat to either Montevideo, their hometown, or to Minneapolis where Duco and Mabel had an apartment at 1211 Franklin Ave. Cleon and Walter finally enlisted the services of Duco, Mabel; Nobel, Blanch, and Margaret. The Franklin Ave. apartment became the gang's headquarters.

The gang became a close entity, a family. Now they had a crowd to party with. The beer and liquor started to flow. On Friday and Saturday nights they would get all liquored up and then go to the club for a night of dancing. They would sometimes stay up for days and party. As long as they stayed home and partied, the public would be safe from their criminal activities. When they were tired of the party it would be time to start planning their next adventure. They would pick out a neighborhood and scope out the newer cars. New cars held the people with big bucks. Usually these neighborhoods would be within walking distance. As a general rule they didn't take the chance of using their cars and having the license plate revealed. Once they spotted a nicer car, they would make their move. They would try and get to the person while he was still in the car Then they would jump in with guns pointed at the victim. If need be, they would pistol slap the victim a bit just to show they were in total control. They had a car and a victim.

They would have the victim drive to a desolate place and park. They would tie and gag the victim and then shove him into the backseat. Cars back then had a rail on the rear seat floorboard. The victim would also be tied to that rail. By now I'm sure the poor person needed a change of clothes.

After getting total control of their prey, they would head back to the apartment and pick up the rest of the gang. They would then head west out of town. After fifty miles or so, they would stop the car and let their prisoner go. He would still have his hands tied and blindfolded, but he would be free.

The gang was emboldened and ready for some robberies. They had a new car, their women were with them, booze or beer, the guns are loaded-- let's go!

Now that's how it was supposed to go down. For nearly a year, this system worked well for them. On the night of February 26, 1933, a Sunday, things were a bit different. They had been drinking for several days. Their downfall began to spin out of control the previous Saturday. All day they sat in the apartment talking and drinking. Later that day they needed some entertainment.

The seven gang members attended a dance Saturday night. They were dancing, laughing, telling stories, and sipping liquor from a flask they smuggled in. They were having a great time. Their party pump was primed. When the dance hall closed they went back to the apartment and continued with the party. They partied all night and into the next day. As the day went on the conversation turned to committing another kidnapping. They were once again ready to snatch another victim and car.

Probably because they were so full of beer and liquor they broke with tradition, and at 5:30 pm, Duco, Waiter, and Nobel left the apartment lot in Duco's car in search of another victim. A short drive later they came upon a new Buick and began to follow it. Eventually the Buick stopped in front of a drugstore at the intersection of 40th Street and Lyndale Ave. S. The owners of the car, Mr. and Mrs. Clay Johnson, had finished dinner at home and decided to go out for an ice cream cone.

The Buick was a new car with a lot of new features. Walter and Nobel were at some loss on the operation of this car. Once they arrived at Fort Snelling, they took turns trying to figure out the mechanics of the car. Mr. Johnson didn't want things to get any worse than what they were, so he decided to teach them the operation of the car. Perhaps the car wouldn't be wrecked during this ordeal. Once the guys had the cars mechanics somewhat figured out, they tied up Mr. Johnson and put him on the backseat floor. They also tied him to the floor rail. Then they headed back to the apartment.

They decided to hold onto Mr. Johnson for a while. They still weren't sure of the car and they might need him to help them. Everyone piled into the car and westward they went. The party that started the day before had new life. The beer and liquor was being served. None for Mr. Johnson, though. As the ladies opened the beer, it sprayed all over the floor and onto Mr. Johnson. When the ladies got excited over a joke or a story, they would stomp their feet with glee. Only one problem with that, they were stomping on Mr. Johnson. If he complained, one of the guys would gun smack him and tell him to shut up. About the only thing that saved him from serious injuries was his dog. Yep, Mr. Johnson had his little dog along and it kept the rear-seated passengers entertained with tricks.

Westward on MN Highway 10 (now MN Highway 12) they went, as fast as that new car would run. They were anxious to make the first robbery. It was decided it would be in Cocato, Minnesota. Traveling through town they noticed a small gas station open a short distance up the road. They slowed to a crawl. As they approached the station the backseat passengers all crouched down on top of Mr. Johnson, nearly suffocating him. They stuck their guns into his face and told him to hold still and shut up or else.

Duco was driving the car with Cleon and Nobel in the front seat with him. As they pulled into the lot, Cleon crouched down in the front. If you looked at the car, it appeared that there were two people in the car. Walter and Nobel were the hold up men. They were in and out of the station in seconds. They performed this so often it became routine. Duco would place the car close to the door for a fast getaway. It worked out great. In just seconds, they netted a couple dollars.

After they got down the road a piece, everyone would pop up and cheer the caper. Beer for everyone! Not you, Mr. Johnson. By now he knew what he was up against; and wondered if he would get out of this alive. He was now a witness to a felony crime. Would the gang let him go with that in mind?

At 10:00 pm Sunday night, Oscar Johnson, Chief of Police in Benson, MN received a call from the Willmar Police Dept. He was informed that two to three men were heading his way in a newer car that had a unique feature of two taillights. Oscar was informed that these people were suspects in hold ups in Cocato, Litchfield, Atwater, and Willmar. He was told that these men were getting more threatening and edgy and they also appeared very intoxicated.

Oscar knew that there are just a few places open on a Sunday along MN Highway 10 this time of night. Coggins Station was one of them. For robbers, it was a perfect location. It was located just on the edge of town and on a major highway.

Another place also came to mind-- Rangaards Cafe. It was located along the highway but it was well lit and usually populated. He also knew that one of his officers was going there for a supper break. Oscar got into his squad and drove to Coggins Station.

When Oscar arrived at Coggins, he hid the squad car in the back of the garage. He walked around to the front door where he met up with Arnie Strand, the night clerk. Oscar put his arm around Arnie's shoulder and guided him back into the store, explaining to him what may happen shortly.

Arnie couldn't believe what he was hearing. It was just two weeks before that he was held up and nearly shot by a hold up man. Arnie made the mistake of whispering under his breath that if he had a gun, he would shoot these robbers. Well, he said it loud enough for one of the gunmen to hear him. The gunman approached him and asked him to repeat what he said and he would shoot him dead on the spot. Arnie did the best thing he could do, he just clammed up. The gunman realized that he regained control and left without further incident.

Oscar was scoping out the station looking for a place to ambush the robbers should they stop there. He told Arnie to call Rangaards Cafe and alert Police Officer Carl Tengvall of the possible problems heading that way. Have him stay at the cafe just in case the robbers decide to rob the cafe.

Arnie called right away. Meanwhile, Oscar couldn't find a real good spot for ambush. He decided to look around outside. He noticed a couple 55-gallon drums in a position that allowed him to observe the front door and the driveway. It was good and dark and it would serve his purpose. He went there, crouched down, and watched for headlights down the highway. It was after 11:00 pm.

Soon he saw a car approach the station. It pulled up to the front door. Arnie was in the store about to panic. He thought Oscar had abandoned him. He wanted out. He bolted to the front door and ran into the gunmen nose-to-nose.

Walter was the first through the door. Pushing Arnie back into the store he said, "Stick 'em up!". With Nobel following Walter into the store they forced Arnie back to the cash register and forced him to open it. Walter asked Arnie, "Did you get that gun yet? Still want to shoot me?"

Arnie nearly passed out. This is the same robber that held him up a few weeks ago. He just kept his mouth shut this time.

While Nobel and Walter were in the store, Oscar decided to arrest the one person he thought was in the car and then use the car for cover against the other two. As he snuck up to the passenger side of the car to give his orders for the driver to put his hands on the wheel, he popped up only to notice that the car had several people in it. He babbled a few incoherent words and reared backward firing his gun at the car. None of the bullets penetrated the car to hit a passenger. He was now in between the car and the front door to the store.

Walter and Nobel heard the shots. They bolted from the front of the store and Arnie ran out the back. Walter came out first firing his gun in every direction. Oscar was crouched down and fired at him once and hit him in the leg. A cry came from the car, "My God, Walter!"

He was able to crawl into the front seat. At that same time, Nobel came out of the store looking for a target to shoot at. Bang, a shot from Oscar's gun hit Nobel in the neck, dropping him dead instantly.

Nobel never fired a shot. Duco was driving. Cleon was sitting next to him. Cleon pulled Walter into the car the rest of the way while Duco floored the car, speeding away from that crazy cop. They went down Highway 12 until they figured they were out of gun range. They took inventory of themselves. Walter had a bullet in his leg and none of them knew if Nobel was dead or alive. They decided that they would have to rescue him. They turned around and headed for the station again. By then, Oscar had moved across the street and took cover. The Buick slowly drove past the station with everyone firing their guns at anything that could hide a person.

At the same time, Oscar opened up from behind them. Stunned, Duco again floored the Buick and got away from there. They stopped at the stockyards a few blocks away to regroup and reload.

In the still of the night, Oscar heard one of them saying, "Give me more shells, I'll get him yet!"

The car approached the station again. Duco tried to maneuver the headlights on Nobel. He ordered everyone to open fire at anything. Now how stupid can a criminal be? Did they forget that Oscar was across the street? They were all firing at the station. Oscar opened up on them again. Duco was satisfied that Nobel was probably dead and he had enough of this crazy cop. He floored the car onto the highway and through Benson.

The shooting wasn't done yet. They still had the gauntlet to run through by the cafe. Carl heard the three salvoes of gunfire. He wondered if Oscar was all right. He didn't want to leave his post so he just waited. The wait paid off for him. He was crouched down near the shoulder of the road when the car approached at a high rate of speed. As they sped past Rangaards Cafe, Carl completely emptied his gun on the car. He shot at the tires.

The gang had quite enough of Benson, MN. The car has been shot up and had at least one flat tire, one person has a bullet in the leg, and one was more than likely dead. This was a bad day. They decided to go to their Montevideo hideout and regroup.

This wasn't the end of this caper. The other half of this night was yet to come. For the gang, it got worse. It didn't go well for a few farmers either.

PHOTO GALLERY

County of .....**Swift**..................) ....**Twelfth**..............*Judicial District.*

THE STATE OF MINNESOTA
AGAINST

.....................**Perley H. Oliva, et al,**.............................

I, ...**K. J. Rodberg,**......................................., *the clerk*

of the above named court, do hereby certify:
      Special
That at a ~~*General*~~ *Term of said court begun on the* ....**13th**.........................*day of*

.**March**...........................*19* **33**., *the Grand Jury duly presented in open court on the*

....**14th**..................*day of* .....**March**.............................*19* **33**, *an indictment against*

.......**Perley H. Oliva, et al,**...............................

charging him with the crime of ....**Robbery in the First Degree**..........................

a true copy of which indictment is hereto attached as a part hereof;
    That on the..........**17th**..........*day of*.....**March**...........*19* **33** *said*

........**Perley H. Oliva,**...............................*was arraigned and entered his plea to said*

indictment, a true copy of which plea is as follows: "**not Guilty**"

That on the 7th. day of April, 1933, Court being in actual session
the Defendant, Perley H. Oliva, with his Attorney, W. W. Merrill, Esq.
appeared in open Court, and at this time petitioned the Court for
leave to withdraw his plea of Not Guilty, and said request having been
granted by the Court, and at this time the said Defendant Perley H.
Oliva, being required to plead to said Indictment, charging him with the
crime of Robbery in the First Degree, "did say" that he was guilty as
charged, Whereafter the said defendant was duly sworn, examined by the
Court before the imposition of sentence, and sentence imposed.

    *That the names and residences of the presiding judge, prosecuting officer, and convict's attorney,
are as follows, to-wit:*
Presiding Judge .....**G. E. Qvale, Willmar, Minnesota**
Prosecuting Officer .....**Kenneth Kivley, Appleton, Minnesota**
Convict's Attorney .....**W. W. Merrill, Montevideo, Minnesota.**
    *That a synopsis furnished by the stenographer acting at said proceeding of the sentence of the
court, said convict's statement under oath, and the statement of the said trial judge of his impressions as
to the mental and physical condition of said convict, his general character, capacity, disposition, habits
and special needs, is hereto attached as a part hereof under the direction of said trial judge.*

    WITNESS, The Honorable..............**G. E. Qvale**...........................*Judge*

of said Court and the seal thereof at .....**Benson, Minnesota** *this* ....**10th.**

County of __Swift__ } __Twelfth__ *Judicial District,*

THE STATE OF MINNESOTA
AGAINST

Mable Oliva, et al,

I, __K. J. Rodberg,__ *, the clerk*

of the above named court, do hereby certify:

That at a __Special__ *Term of said court began on the* __13th__ *day of* __March__ 19 __33__, *the Grand Jury duly presented in open court on the* __14th__ *day of* __March__ 19 __33__, *an indictment against* __Mable Oliva, et al,__

charging her *with the crime of* __Kidnapping__

a true copy of which indictment is hereto attached as a part hereof;

That on the __17th__ *day of* __March__ 19 __33__, *said* __Mable Oliva,__ *was arraigned and entered* her *plea to said indictment, a true copy of which plea is as follows:* "Not Guilty"

That on the 7th day of April, 1933, Court being convened in Actual session, the said defendant Mable Oliva, with her Attorney, W. W. Merrill Esq. appeared in open Court, and at this time petitioned the Court for granted by the Court, and at this time the said defendant being before the Court, and being required to plead to the said Indictment charging her with the crime of Kidnapping, did say that she was guilty as charged Whereafter the said defendant was duly sworn, examined by the Court before the imposition of sentence, and sentence imposed,

That the names and residences of the presiding judge, prosecuting officer, and convict's attorney, are as follows, to-wit:

Presiding Judge __G. E. Qvale, Willmar, Minnesota__

Prosecuting Officer __Kenneth Kivley, Appleton, Minnesota__

Convict's Attorney __W. W. Merrill, Montevideo, Minnesota.__

That a synopsis furnished by the stenographer acting at said proceeding of the sentence of the court, said convict's statement under oath, and the statements of the said trial judge of his impressions as to the mental and physical condition of said convict, his general character, capacity, disposition, habits and special needs, is hereto attached as a part hereof under the direction of said trial judge.

WITNESS, The Honorable __G. E. Qvale__ *Judge of said Court and the seal thereof at* __Benson, Minnesota__ *this* __10th__ *day of* __April__ 19 __33__

Be It Hereby Known,

WHEREAS, The Board of Parole of the Minnesota State Prison
has certified to me that one PERLEY H. OLIVA
who was convicted of the crime of ROBBERY, FIRST DEGREE
in SWIFT *County, and sentenced to imprisonment in the*
State Prison on the 10th *day of* APRIL 1933,
was released on a conditional parole on the 29th *day of*
MAY *1939, and granted his final release to take effect on the*
14th *day of* MAY 1941
Now, Therefore, I HAROLD E. STASSEN *Governor of*
the State of Minnesota, pursuant to law do hereby restore the said
PERLEY H. OLIVA *to all the civil rights,*
which were forfeited by his conviction and sentence.

In Witness Whereof, I have hereunto set my
hand and caused the Great Seal of the State
to be affixed at the Capitol, in the City of
St. Paul, this SIXTEENTH
day of MAY *A. D. 19* 41

HAROLD E. STASSEN

By the Governor.

MIKE HOLM

Secretary of State.

2781

34

This is a 1933 Buick. It would be similar to the car
that the Bonrud Gang comandeered from Clay
Johnson in front of the drug store in Minneapolis.
The car did in fact have two tail lights as described
by the Wilmer Police to the Benson Police. This was
unique for the time.

Honorable Men

These are the two lawmen that stopped the Bonrud Gang and put them in custody.

On the right is Benson's Police Chief Oscar Johnson. The shootout at Coggins Station more than confused the gang. He was able to shoot and kill Nobel Bonrud and wound Walter Christenson. Police Officer Carl Tengvall also took a few shots at the car while it was escaping from town.(He's not pictured) His shots punctured the rear tires.

Pictured on the left is Chippewa County Sheriff Nels Peterson. After being alerted to the activity at Benson he gathered a posse and drove north towards Benson to head off the gang. Half way they encountered the gang. After a few shots were fired the gang surrendered. They were jailed at the more secure Montevideo jail.

Dads 80th Birthday 8/2/2004 Patty, Ken,
Cheryl, Jack, and Linda

Darlos 1934 "A Look of Despair"

Mabel, Duco, Mavis and Darlos
1932

Jack and Darlos She had less than three
months to live.

Mavis and Darlos 1929

Mavis, Darlos, and Mabel 1972

Duco 1963

Mabel in Nursing Home 1989

Duco, Ken and Mabel 1963

Duco with a 9lb. 13oz. Walley
caught on Mille Lac 1968

Darlos on a good day in 1968

ARRESTED

They were racing out of town as fast as that fancy Buick would go. I can only imagine their panicked thinking at this time; what's wrong with that cop shooting at us like that? Nobody ever shot at us before. My God, what about Nobel? He must be dead; we didn't see him move at all. He just dropped like a tree. ~~Damn~~ Walter, are you all right? Is anybody hit in the backseat? No. OK! My God, Duco, get us ~~the hell~~ out of here.

The Bonrud Gang knew this area fairly well. They were raised in Chippewa and Swift counties and often traveled to the nearby towns for teenage action. On these roads, the most people ever saw was a farmhouse every mile or so. The roads were all gravel and minimally maintained by today's standards. They wanted to get to Monte, short for Montevideo, and hide out for a while. At least until the heat was off. They had family and friends there, sympathizers to their activities. These people had been beat up hard by the Depression. It always seemed like it was the farmers that came in last at the food line. Most of the family and friends were farmers. Any anti-establishment activities were fine with them. Taking persons new Buick smelled like big money to them. They knew the big money nested with the establishment. The gang could explain everything to their family.

That February was warm and the frost was moving up in the roadway, making it muddy and slippery. The car was swaying more than usual. Duco found a spot to pull off the road and hide behind some trees. When they all got out inspecting the car and stretching their legs, it was noticed that the car had two flat tires. They both had bullet holes. They were kind of screwed. Two flat tires and only one spare. They needed another car.

They figured they should stay away from Clontarf as it was a sure bet that the police there have been notified of the shootout and they were just itching to take shots at the gang. It was decided that Cleon, Margaret, and Walter with his bad leg would roam to some farmhouse and get a car. It was darker than most nights, and electricity hadn't reached all the farming communities yet. Farmhouses were hard to spot without the familiar yard light. It was about midnight.

The three of them walked for what they thought were miles until they came up to Henry Larson's farm. The three banged on the door until Henry answered. Cleon explained that they had car trouble and would pay him to drive them to a hotel in town. Henry could use the extra money, so he agreed. He got dressed.

Once inside the car, Cleon requested that Henry take them back to their broken car and retrieve some clothes. Henry agreed and asked for directions to the car. Cleon was totally lost. Walter spoke up and pointed down the road in a direction that he really wasn't sure of. Henry complied and drove off in that direction.

The gangsters didn't realize that they were back on the road to Benson. They saw city lights, but they thought it was Clontarf. They figured it would be okay to drive there because they were in a local person's car.

Everyone knew everyone around there. As they got closer to the city they noticed that it was Benson. Whoa! Turn the car around, Henry!

Henry was startled. He looked at his passengers and saw two guns pointed right between his eyes. Henry stopped the car. Walter pulled up his pant leg, revealing the bullet hole and Cleon shoved his gun into Henry's nose.

Walter said, "Look, we're in one heck of a fix here and we need your help."

Henry agreed to anything, especially with guns pointed at him.

Cleon said, "Take us towards Clontarf. We need to find our car."

He obliged the gunmen and turned the car around. Instead of heading toward Clontarf Henry was driving north towards Lake Hassel. One of the gunmen was concerned about the lack of city lights. Being suspicious he ordered Henry to take the next road to the right. Henry stated that, "Taking the next right will take us around Lake Hassel." "The early warm weather has caused the road to be flooded and we could get stuck".

Cleon edged his gun into Henry's rib and said, "It would be bad for you if we get stuck."

Henry turned his car down the road they wanted. He traveled a few blocks and sure enough, the car got stuck.

Henry had a shot of adrenaline and barked at the guys, "Now damn it, I've had enough of you guys pushing me around. I won't go any farther with you."

This kind of startled the guys and they believed him. They didn't want to push a car out of mud anyway. They saw a farm about a quarter mile back. They would get another car there.

Cleon got a bit upset over Henry's little speech. He got out of the car and came around to the driver's door and opened it. He grabbed Henry and pulled him out of the car. He shoved the gun in his ribs and said, "You're coming with me." He told the others to stay put.

Cleon figured that Henry knew the people in the farmhouse. Henry did know them.

Cleon said that they need another car and if he said anything to prevent that from happening, he would shoot everyone in the house. They got to the farmhouse and knocked on the door.

Aroused from sleep, Ed Wayne got out of bed and looked out the window and saw his neighbor Henry. *Very curious*, he thought, went downstairs, and opened the door.

Cleon pushed Henry through the doorway and then thrust the gun into Ed's face and told him, "I need you to help me find my friends, and then you're going to drive us all out of this forsaken country!"

Ed saw that the gangster was desperate and agreed to help.

Cleon told Henry to stay put. If Henry did anything stupid, Cleon said he would return to kill him. Ed and Cleon got into Ed's car and took off. First, they retrieved Margaret and Walter, then Cleon gave Ed the best hints he could think of to locate the others. Ed immediately had an idea where the car was hidden.

Meanwhile, back at the Wayne farm, Leland and Logan Wayne woke from a sleep and were taken by surprise to see Henry sitting at the kitchen table. Henry explained everything that happened to him. He told the brothers that these guys didn't have any problems shoving guns in his face. He also said that he believed them when they said that they would shoot him. It was decided that the three of them would arm themselves and go to the Viking Cafe in Clontarf and call the police. Then the brothers thought again, Ed has the only car they all own. The gangsters have control of it now.

Henry said he could drive. It was the only choice. They all agreed and started to hike toward Henry's car. When they got to Henry's car they told Henry to get in and they would push him out of the mud.

Henry said, "Get in, the car isn't really stuck! I just pretended to be stuck so I could ditch those guys." Henry turned the car around and headed for Clontarf.

When they got to the Viking Café, they called the Benson Police. Henry told Oscar that the gang wanted to get to Montevideo but for now they were searching for the rest of the gang. He couldn't be sure where they were, however.

After much driving around, Ed had located the broken down car hiding behind some trees. As they parked the car, Mabel and Blanch ran toward Cleon and Walter, happy that they came back.

"Where is Duco?" asked Cleon.

Mabel blurted out that he walked up to a schoolhouse up the road a piece. The two women got into Ed's car along with Cleon and Walter and they drove to the school to pick up Duco. They would then force Ed to drive the back roads to Montevideo.

Meanwhile, the new Buick was abandoned behind the trees with Mr. Johnson still tied up in the backseat. He would eventually work himself free.

At about the same time, the Benson Police Chief Oscar Johnson, called Chippewa County Sheriff Nels Peterson in Montevideo and told him that he had a major shootout with some dangerous people. He said there was one dead and another wounded. Chief Johnson stated he wasn't sure how many were in the car, but he guessed about six or seven. He said they all had guns and they all used them against him.

Nels immediately called Montevideo Police Chief L. Skunkberg and Police volunteer Arthur Tinson. Both shook off their sleep and sped to the Sheriff's Department in Monte and met up with the sheriff. These law enforcement officers boarded the sheriff's car and headed north out of town on Highway 38 to Benson. The gang shot at a law enforcement officer. There is nothing worse in the minds of the police than that. If these people will shoot at the lawmen, they wouldn't hesitate to shoot a citizen. This posse was on a mission: arrest this gang. They were armed and extremely dangerous.

Back at the abandoned Buick, Mr. Johnson was able to free himself. He picked up his dog, shoved it under his coat, and started walking toward the city lights. It was now close to 2:00 am. If a car happened to come along, he would dive into the ditch and hide. He wasn't sure if the gang was out looking for him. He decided to climb a small incline and walk the railroad tracks. He felt safe there.

A short walk later, he came onto the Ludwig Peterson farm. He politely knocked on the door. When Ludwig answered the door, he could see the man standing at his door was in distress. He grabbed the stranger's arm and led him into the house. He sat him down in the kitchen and immediately put on a pot of coffee. Minnesota hospitality, you have to admire it. After some conversation and coffee to warm the bones, Mr. Johnson stated that he would like to make some phone calls. Ludwig didn't have a phone but offered to drive him to the Paris Hotel in Benson. They had a phone.

The two men arrived at the Paris Hotel and Mr. Johnson explained his situation to the night clerk. The hotel clerk gave Mr. Johnson whatever he needed, including the phone.

Mr. Johnson called three people. He first called his wife, then Benson Police Chief Oscar, and finally his law firm partners. As it turned out, Mr. Clay Johnson was a partner in the very prestigious law firm Fowler, Carlson, Fuber and Johnson. This law firm had clout. It had a close relationship with a United States Attorney G.A.Younquist. The US Attorney would hand overflow cases out to the law firm.

The law firm worked closely and often with the police departments in Minneapolis and St. Paul. They worked even closer to the Minnesota Bureau of Criminal Apprehension.

On the phone call with his wife, Mr. Johnson learned that after she purchased the ice cream cones, she walked outside to notice him speeding away. She had a strong feeling that he was kidnapped.

This is a good time to mention a bit of information about the rash of kidnappings across the country. After the kidnapping and death of Baby Lindberg, a new law was forced through Congress addressing the issue of kidnapping. Charles Lindberg was instrumental in lobbying for the passage of the federal law named "The Lindbergh Kidnapping Law". It was now a federal offense to commit kidnapping and when caught and convicted, the sentence is a minimum twenty years in prison. The FBI was also authorized to investigate kidnappings.

Kidnapping was so prevalent and frequent; these ads ran in all editions of all major newspapers across the country. "Kidnapping is now a Federal offense punishable by 20 years in federal prison and up to a $10,000 fine". After a while it seemed to have worked. Later in 1932, the kidnapping rate lowered. Federal prosecutors sent fewer people to federal prisons and not the cushy state prisons.

While talking to his wife, Mr. Johnson learned of his wife's efforts to locate her husband. After she called his close friend, Mr. Comaford, he promised to bring all law enforcement personnel to bear on this horrible crime against his best friend. He was true to his word. It goes to show you that big money has clout in high places. At this time in the morning, 2:00 am, Mr. Comaford called Minneapolis Police Chief William J. Meehan, Police Secretary

George Fenney, and Melvin Passholt of the Minnesota Bureau of Criminal Apprehension.

Of course, all these important high-ranking officials brought in all their people and instruments to bear on this gang. I'd say that the low profiled Bonrud Gang has been enjoying their crime sprees just a bit longer than they should have. The city and state officials have lawyers nipping at them and forcing them to take drastic measures that will be in the open for all to see. This gang will be exposed and penalized as a warning to all. There will be no more cuddling up with gangsters.

Back in the getaway car, Ed was taking all the back roads he could think of trying to get to Montevideo. He kept telling the gang that staying on the gravel roads would sooner or later swallow the car's tires. The gang had enough of searching for new vehicles and they weren't in any mood to push a stuck car out of the mud. Cleon gave him permission to get on Highway 38 and beat feet to Montevideo. Ed was relieved and he soon came to Highway 38 and turned south toward Montevideo. He drove as fast as that car would go. He just wanted to get there and get these desperadoes out of his car. He wanted this to end peacefully without incident. He was terrified, but who wouldn't be?

I think he was justified in feeling this way. The gang was out of control. I'm not so sure they would leave a witness alive after they were dropped at their hideout. At this point in time, Ed's life was in extreme danger.

Unknown to the Bonrud Gang at the time, the posse from Montevideo was speeding north on Highway 38. After a few minuets, the cars passed each other on the highway. Sheriff Peterson had a hunch about that vehicle immediately. Who else would be speeding toward Monte at this time in the morning?

He turned his squad car around and charged toward the gangsters' vehicle. The sheriff's squad car was, of course, built specially for the police. This squad was a high-powered pursuit vehicle with special suspension and tires all built for speed. It also had a professionally trained driver at the wheel.

It didn't take long for the sheriff's car to catch up to Ed's car. The sheriff maneuvered his squad car up next to the speeding car with the gangsters. The lawmen were aware that the driver was Ed and they would take all precautions not to hurt him in the arrest. Once the two cars were side-by-side, the lawmen opened fire on the gangsters, trying to aim away from Ed. Dozens of bullets was flying in and around the gangsters' car. Side-by-side they were speeding down the highway. The lawmen were somewhat taken aback when they realized that the bad guys were not shooting back. In fact, they had their hands raised. I'm sure the lawmen had a collective thought, "What's up with that? We thought you were real tough guys. You're not going to shoot back?"

To the lawmen's surprise, one of the women in the backseat was waving a white handkerchief out the rear window. He could read her lips, "We surrender!"

The cars eventually came to a stop on the roadway. Once they were stopped, the lawmen jumped out of their squad and took the offensive posture. Also at this time, a Benson reinforcement police officer Ed Flatten arrived at the scene and also took an offensive position. The gang was surrounded and facing enough gunfire that could tear them to pieces.

The lawmen shouted orders at the gang simultaneously. . I'm sure adrenaline was overflowing in the lawmen's veins. The sheriff fired two pistol shots in the air just to prove his point that he wasn't going to grant any liberties. This scared the hell out of the gangsters. No matter what, they decided to comply with the sheriff's orders. It was a classic police takedown.

One at a time the lawmen ordered the gang to get out of the car. They were all eventually handcuffed and put under arrest. It was over. The sheriff decided that the gang should be held at his Chippewa County Jail in Montevideo. It was a larger facility with good security. There was no argument from Benson officials. They just had a small town one-cell jail. They were happy to let Chippewa County assume custody.

On the way to Monte, five of the gang members rode with Sheriff Peterson in his squad car. The other two would ride in the Benson's police car with Ed Flatten at the wheel.

With five members riding with the sheriff, Skunkberg and Tinsman stood on the squad's step rails all the way to jail. They hung onto the car with one hand and trained their pistols on the five gang members with the other hand.

The night of terrorism was over. The gang was going to jail. The citizens were now safe from the Bonrud Gang.

Well, not so fast with that thinking. Remember, this was the gang's home turf. They had many friends and sympathizers in the area. I wouldn't count them out until they are convicted and sent to prison.

The Bonrud Gang was now being held in the Chippewa County Jail in Montevideo, Minnesota. A few hours before they'd wanted to be in Montevideo, but not like this. Each and every one of them knew that they were in serious trouble; very serious trouble. They knew about the Lindbergh Kidnapping Law, and they knew they could get up to twenty years each in prison. How did things go so wrong? How on Earth did that cop in Benson get to us the way he did? How could they unload so many bullets on one man and not even scratch him?

How he was able to keep composed enough to fire his weapon and wound one in the leg and skillfully place a bullet through the neck of Nobel, killing him? Who was that copper?

How stupid were we to be so panicked that we missed the turn to Montevideo and on top of it all, lose track of where we parked the Buick? If we would have kept our heads, perhaps we would have made a clean getaway to Montevideo and stayed at the hide out. Our family would have provided for us until things cooled down. Just how stupid are we?

I think stupid is only part of the reason. How about a brain full of alcohol? It has to be remembered that Mr. Johnson said that they were drinking all the way. As the women opened beer for the men, the spray would soak him while he was tied to the back seat floor rail. Were they so naïve as to think that drinking didn't contribute to their capture? There are no court documents mentioning alcohol as a contributing factor. Today, well let's just say if you're caught under these circumstances, one of the very first things a police officer will do is pull out his PBT (portable breath tester) and make you blow into it. Statistics on alcohol related crimes are kept and analyzed by several groups of law enforcement and scientist.

They each had time to ponder their foolishness. They were going to have plenty of time to think about everything, maybe even escape.

The new law was a great new tool for the local police. The authorities were going to make the Bonrud Gang their poster child. Other gangs had better pay attention to this. It wasn't going to be pretty.

Not only was a new law going to be used but now the law firm would expose to the public to all the negative things that come from associating and consorting with hard core criminals. They knew the internal policies the police had when it came to ignoring the big time criminals and granting them safe haven. Their campaign has begun and their focus was going to be that gang that kidnapped their partner.

Minneapolis Police Chief Meehan, Minneapolis Police Secretary Fenney, and Agent Passholt of the Minnesota Bureau of Criminal Apprehension heard the news of the capture of the gang and the safe release of Clay Johnson from the law firm. The firm made sure they were notified, and they informed the officials that they would be watching. The lawmen felt this pressure and they responded immediately. They were in their squads and heading for Montevideo. Now is the time to set an example of what can happen when serious crimes were committed in Minneapolis. The days of safe haven for anyone were over. If the Bonrud Gang did anything constructive, it would be the surfacing and public scrutiny of the safe haven policy the Twin Cities had with the hardcore criminals. It is a new beginning for law enforcement in the Twin Cities.

Back in the county jail, Blanch was going through a grieving period. Her man, Nobel, was dead. Blanch was young, naïve, and impressionable. She was small in stature and was the "cute little one" of the group. She was the baby of the group and was constantly trying to act an age beyond her 18 years. Nobel swept her off her feet and gave her anything her little heart desired. She left home at an early age and was totally influenced by Nobel. She would do anything for him, and was totally dependant on him for everything. Now he was gone. Depression set in deep and hard. The reality set in and she became pale and worried looking. No longer the young bubbly girl she was a couple hours ago, she started believing that without Nobel to protect her, the gang would place all the blame on her. They would make her the ringleader. She knew if this were to happen she would take the full load of punishment from the court. Blanch talked herself into a place where only she could get herself out of. She had to confess and tell her story first.

Sheriff Peterson was keeping a close eye on her. He went as far as to put her in an isolation cell. He told her that the Minneapolis and Minnesota officials were on their way to talk with her. The sheriff has seen this behavior before. He knew exactly what to do, take advantage of it. Blanch became so paranoid that she finally broke down and told the sheriff that she had information about other crimes. She would trade this information for leniency. The sheriff knew that he had her right where he wanted her but he wanted her to wait and tell her story to the Minneapolis and State officials.

Meehan, Fenney, and Passholt finally arrived mid morning. Sheriff Peterson told them that Blanch was the insecure one and wanted to talk. The investigators were a bit taken aback by her willingness to talk. Usually gang members were so tight with each other; they would rather die than squeal on each other.

Collectively they thought, if she wants to talk, we better get it while it's hot. This case may be easier than we thought.

They brought Blanch into an interview room. They offered her beverages and cigarettes. They wanted her comfortable. Their first questions were, "Who the hell are you people?" "Where did you all come from?" "Are there any more of you we should know about?"

Blanch answered the questions as fast as they could ask them. In between the questions, she would break down and cry. She had a big load on her shoulders and it was taking its toll.

She was in a daze. She was just offering information on other crimes committed recently that Minneapolis Police had no clues on how to solve them. Blanch mentioned a recent crime where they kidnapped a Mr. Heck from the intersection of Franklin Ave. and Chicago Ave. in Minneapolis.

They bound and gagged him, tossed him into the backseat of his own car, they laid him on the floor, and tied him to the rail. They drove off and went to St. Louis Park, a western suburb, where they robbed him, and then abandoned him and the car. They hot wired another car that was nearby and drove off to Norseland, MN.

They pulled into a gas station and robbed it. They kidnapped the attendant and stole his car.

Then they drove to Cedar Rapids, Iowa. Here the gang abandoned the attendant and car and nabbed another victim and his car. They drove deeper into Iowa and eventually released their victim. They also relieved him of all his valuables.

They kept the car and drove it back to Minneapolis. There was no real purpose to this trip. It was just an adventure that played out as it happened. The gang would perform these crimes with a child like mood. They enjoyed the terror they could express onto their hapless victims. At times it was more like a game to them. After all, what was there to be afraid of, the gang had the guns. It wasn't a game now, and it certainly isn't fun.

The investigators were stunned. So many crimes cleared up in just a short period of time.

What a stroke of good fortune. They had no idea that a gang was operating out of Minnesota with such proficiency.

"Just who the hell are you people?"

The investigators left the interview room so they could take a breath. They were beside themselves. How could these small time hoodlums operate like this and get away with it? Could there be more of them? If so, Blanch wasn't saying anything about it. These few people just couldn't be the only members. This gang had to be bigger. They thought she was protecting more gang members back in Minneapolis.

It was decided that they would call headquarters back in Minneapolis and have them arrange an invasion on the apartment on Franklin Ave. Chief Meehan informed his subordinates to be careful. These people were armed and extremely dangerous. He advised that they should use at least 24 officers in this raid. The members they had in custody had no hesitation shooting it out with the police and if there are more of them in that apartment, they might want a shoot out too.

The Minneapolis Police officer in charge followed his leader's orders to the letter. They arrived at the apartment with twelve squad cars with two officers in each one. They bumbled their way up the stairs and rammed the door down in a cadence like motion. They rushed in with guns drawn, barking orders to people who weren't there. They searched the place inside out; all they found was a terrorized twelve-year-old Mavis Peterson. She was the older of two daughters from Mabel. Mavis had been living there alone. The raid on her home scared her. She was crying uncontrollably. The 24 officers were totally taken back when they discovered this 12 year old being left alone. They also felt bad that they had to take such an action to enter the apartment the way they did and scare the girl nearly senseless.

The police officers took Mavis to the station and interviewed her in the most sensitive manner possible. The police learned that she was left alone many times and for many days at a time. Her mom would leave food and some change for her to spend at the candy store. Asking her about other family members she mentioned that if she had an emergency, she could ask her aunt Manda for help. The police considered this an emergency and called Manda.

She and her husband Clarence immediately drove to the police station and took custody of Mavis. Before Mavis left with her aunt, she asked the captain, "Why did you break down the door and raid her home?" He told her that her mother was in jail in Montevideo for kidnapping. Mavis cried out, "No, my mother couldn't do anything wrong!"

The next day that quote was front page news in all the Minneapolis and St. Paul papers.

The Bonrud Gang had been exposed to the public.

The captain of the raiding group called Chief Meehan in Montevideo and reported his findings, "There was nothing there but a twelve-year-old girl."

For the time being everything was under control. The investigation by all the authorities was continuing. The gang was confined and under control. They requested to have visitors, but the request was denied until the Sheriff could sort things out on the local level. He was suspicious why the gang wanted to get to Monte. He would eventually get his answer, and it would nearly be a total embarrassment to his office.

On February 28, 1933, the Swift County Coroner conducted an inquest into the shooting death of Nobel Bonrud. Chief Oscar Johnson was completely exonerated. It was officially declared that, "Nobel Bonrud was shot and killed by Police Chief Oscar Johnson while in the performance of his lawful duty." That was all that needed to be said back then.

Today an officer must prove that his or someone else's life is in imminent danger of great bodily harm or death. Oscar would have passed that test too. He could have been killed just as easily as Nobel. The gangsters carried guns for a reason.

During his testimony at the Inquest, Oscar claimed that when he searched the body he recovered $4.00 in cash, a few wristwatches, and a pistol. He also noted in his report that the pistol was not fired. Oscar claimed to have fired nine rounds during the whole shootout.

I believe that Oscar was the hero of the year. All by himself he took on seven members of a violent gang. He didn't back away and run from the danger, he performed his duty well above the call. It could have gone bad for him real quick when the gangsters turned around twice and charged his position. Oscar stood fast and performed his duty magnificently. I never found out if Oscar was decorated for his courage that night. He should have been. Perhaps an official in Benson reading this memoir could take the steps needed to posthumously award Chief Oscar Johnson. He certainly deserves the public recognition.

At the time of the shootout I believe the gang took their violence to another level. They were on a frenzy fueled by stupidity and alcohol. The successful robberies along the way to Benson embolden them and hand guns made them ten feet tall. I'm convinced that they would have eventually killed someone. They tried to murder a police officer. Not only did the gang make two more passes at Oscar, they were planning on murdering him. Now in my way of thinking this has become intent. Oscar claimed he heard one of them say that, "he needed more shells and he would get him yet." Let's put this into real perspective. I would have thought that saying "he would get him yet" would be a plan to kill a police officer. They could have driven away. The choice they made was to murder Oscar. Granted, it was the testimony of one, but it was the intended victim that gave the testimony. Charges of attempted 1st degree murder were never mentioned. 2nd degree attempted murder charges were never mentioned, as a matter of fact, there was no assault charges at all pertaining to any violence committed towards the Police Chief. When Duco was released from prison, a newspaperman asked him, "What would you have done different that night?" His response, "I would have killed the witnesses." How profound is that?

Joseph Bonrud, a surviving family brother, attended the inquest. He was also there to identify the body and then escort it to Baxter, Minnesota for burial. His attendance had to be hard on him. He sat through the whole Grand Jury process. Once Nobel's body was released to him, he couldn't get out of town fast enough.

A few days later, the Bonrud family conducted a funeral for Nobel in Baxter Minnesota. The family was huge and there were also many friends. The gathering was a bit intimidating to the local law enforcement. These people were sympathetic towards the gang's activities. Why they sympathized with the gang was a hot button issue of the time. The family was fed up with Government and big business control of the country. Any gang that would act against either of them were martyrs in their minds. They were misguided and lied to by the gang. It's obvious the gang spoon fed miss-information to their family. The more the gang could make themselves look good in the eyes of the family, the more the gang could rely on their help. When the gang came to this area after a spree of crime, they could count on the family to feed and house them.

At the funeral among the attendees were twelve-year-old Mavis and her little six-year-old sister Darlos. Now Darlos was a surprise for the cops. They didn't know anything about her until the funeral. They learned that she was indeed the youngest daughter belonging to Mabel. It was also learned that Mabel would count on her sister Carrie to take care of Darlos on the farm outside Montevideo for weeks at a time.

Mabel was allowed to attend the funeral. She was escorted by heavily-armed guards. She was shadowed by her keepers everywhere she went. She arrived late and missed the service but caught the burial. As she walked past her daughters she cried out, "My babies, oh my babies!"

This outburst caused her immediate removal. The guards literally picked her up and tossed her into the Paddy Wagon. This bit of information made the Twin Cities newspapers. People were talking about the woman that left her kids for crime. Others were mad with a woman that would scream such a saying and yet abandon them for a night of crime. It was obvious; Mabel was going to play her girls against the Judge and any sentencing she might get. She would show the public that she was a caring mom. It worked to a degree. She fooled some of the people, but not all. The people that believed Mabel was misguided were later outnumbered by people that were convinced that she didn't deserve to have her daughters. It was determined that she was a gang member that really spurred the rest of the gang on. Not so much the leader, but more of a cheerleader. Mabel actually never scored many points with her family. She was bossy and self absorbing. The only people that could stand her were in the gang.

The guards couldn't get away from the funeral scene fast enough. They were concerned that sympathizers would try and grab her. If the guards only knew what most of us knew about Mabel, she was a drama queen. Actually as far as some of the family was concerned, the cops could keep her.

Back at the jail, the boys learned that Blanch was confessing. They began thinking that it could be to their advantage if they all told the truth. Maybe there could be some leniency on sentencing; they wanted to talk to Passholt.

After listening to the prisoners, Passholt told them he was powerless to grant any favors, however, he would mention in his reports that the gang members became cooperative and wanted to repent. It was the best he could offer.

The gang figured they had nothing to lose. They had a lot of weight on their shoulders and the wanted to get rid of it. They collectively thought; "Ok, let's confess our crimes." One by one, Passholt took them into the interview room. At first he just couldn't believe what he was hearing. Right off the bat, Cleon admitted to 43 different kidnappings and armed robberies. Each subsequent person he talked to admitted the same crimes.

Passholt was stunned. He cleared up more cases in one hour than he cleared in his whole career.

Two days later, the gang wanted to talk again with Passholt. He agreed and took them all at once into the interview room. They admitted to 21 more crimes. Again, they were kidnappings and armed robberies.

Passholt couldn't believe what he was hearing. He asked the gang if they would sign confessions, "This could go a long way in the judge's eyes. He may be easier on you." Everyone agreed to sign. Passholt had a transcriber write up the confessions. It took a couple of hours. Passholt was worried that they may cool off and change their minds be for the transcripts were done.

When the documents were finished, the gang nearly got into a fight trying to be the first to sign. The lawmen were just flabbergasted.

In the lawmen's eyes, this case was closed. So were 64 other cases. Solving crimes in this manner is what dreams are made of. They had no idea a gang with so much moxie was operating in Minneapolis. How could law enforcement let them get through the system without notice? Two of them were career criminals with prison records. They just slipped between the cracks and out of sight.

Policies and procedures were going to change in Minneapolis and at the State Department of Criminal Apprehension. Those high profile killers were not welcome anymore. If this small town gang could get away with over 64 crimes, what could those professional killers get away with?

As evidence of a crack down, on March 30, 1934, information was received at the St. Paul Police Department and the Minneapolis office of the FBI that John Dillenger was hold up at Lincoln Court Apartments in St. Paul. The FBI office sent agents to the apartment building and watched it for a short time. It was soon determined that Dillenger was indeed there. It was time to capture Dillenger. The FBI with just a couple agents made their move. They entered the building and approached Dillengers apartment door. They didn't bother knocking, they rammed the door down and confronted a shotgun armed Dillenger in his apartment. A shootout was started by Dillenger as he shot his way out a rear window for escape. The authorities didn't plant a surveillance team around the apartment's perimeter and Dillenger made a successful escape. Not all was lost however; Dillenger was now sporting a bullet wound to his leg. He escaped to Mooresville, Indiana. The FBI felt good about not hesitating in rooting out this spree killer and either killing him or running him out of town. This was a positive move in the eyes of the general public. The public was starting to gain confidence in their law enforcement again.

With the dramatic ousting of Dillenger by the short handed FBI, other gangs that took refuge in Minnesota were having second thoughts. Granted, Dillenger got away sporting a bullet in the leg, but the gangs knew the turn out could have been different. The FBI could just as easily shot and killed him. With that, Minneapolis and St. Paul was cleared of all the major gangs. Now the authorities could pay attention to any local gang activity.

Kid Cann (September 8, 1900 – June 21, 1981,) was a local mob king pin in Minneapolis. Up until the time that the Bonrud gang was caught, he was afforded the luxury of freedom to move about without police interference. Extortion was his favored illegal activity. He has been accused of attempted murder and murder numerous times. He had ties to a huge Mafia Godfather named Genovese who was based in Chicago. Crimes organized between the two of them resulted in a fat bank account for both of them. Also at the time the governor of Minnesota, Floyd Olson, was being investigated by the FBI for alleged ties to Kid Cann in criminal activities. With all this investigative heat put on Kid Cann, he decided to move to Miami. Once in Miami he hooked up with Meyer Lansky and together they operated a profitable crime gang. Eventually the heat was too hot in Miami and Kid Cann moved back to Minneapolis. By then Minneapolis was tearing down the street car operation and replacing it with busses. Kid Cann maneuvered his way in to steel some of the scrap iron and cash it in with recyclers. It's thought he made millions on the street cars scrap iron. Had authorities been more on the ball, those millions of dollars could have gone a long way in helping the citizens in the Twin Cities with their re-growth and infrastructure. I wonder this, just how big does an item need to be for any police officer to see it's being stolen? Those street cars were big and yellow! How can you possibly steal them without some inside help?

MABEL FAINTS IN COURT

Minnesota's own Bonrud Gang made big time news throughout the five state regions. Minnesota, North Dakota, South Dakota, Iowa, and Wisconsin all took notice of the reported gang activity. Border city cops were combing through their open cases with hope of solving some of their crimes. Certainly with the gang admitting to over 64 crimes, some of those had to be committed in their town. If there were a winner in this, it would have been Iowa. Several armed holdups and kidnappings were committed there. It came as a great relief to those towns that had open cases. They could now close them and consider them solved. It had an extra benefit for the fringe states; Minnesota would be conducting the expensive trials and putting up the expense of incarcerating them for years to come. None of the other states were demanding the prisoners be sent to them for trial and punishment.

Being that the major activities of the recent crimes were committed in Benson, Minnesota, Swift County would be the presiding venue. Shooting at a police officer certainly qualified Swift County to conduct the trial. Benson just happened to be the city where the county seat stood. Swift County at the time was mostly a farming community. After enduring the drought and the economic crash in the stock markets, farmers were experiencing hard times. They felt that they were the lowest on the food chain to receive FDR's benefits from the New Deal. Foreclosures on farms were at an all-time high. Banks were failing left and right from foreclosures. Swift County was a poor county, very poor.

One thing that made Swift County stand out above the rest was their pride in keeping their self-esteem throughout that horrible national crisis. They were not going to let a bunch of city slickers march into their county and threaten public officials and the public in general. This county was about to set an example for all to see. There will be a judicial process that's according to law. These people will be tried in a court of law and represented by council. There will be no slip-ups during this trial. The Swift County pride was at stake. Their name would certainly be represented in newspapers nationwide. They wanted a positive review of the county.

As evidence of the poor economic situation in Swift County, the police and sheriff departments had to make a deal with Chippewa County to hold the prisoners in their jail. Benson just didn't have a jail secure enough, or large enough to hold this gang. Chippewa County was very obliging with Swift County but insisted that Swift County conduct the trials. All parties were in agreement. The prisoners had no voice in any of this. Actually, how could they avoid it? They tried to kill their Chief of Police. Kidnapping a couple farmers didn't help the gang's cause either. They stepped into the pile very deep. They would be lucky to get through this alive. The tension in the air was getting thick.

Finally on March 13 and 14, 1933, a special session of the Swift County Grand Jury convened in the Benson court house. All six members of the Bonrud Gang were indicted on kidnapping charges and attempted armed robbery charges. These proceedings were conducted in secret. The general public couldn't sit in on these proceedings. Probable cause and evidence were entered and displayed to the Grand Jury by the District Attorney. The Judge sat and monitored the proceedings and made sure that everything presented was in accordance to law. The Grand Jury needed to hear and see evidence that just balanced the evidence enough to warrant an arraignment hearing. The Grand Jury, under advice from the judge, could determine what charges should be levied against the defendants.

On Tuesday, March 21, 1933 the gang was ordered to appear for the first time in Benson to answer the charges against them. It was their time to plead guilty or not guilty. The court proceedings were going to be a spectacular event. The logistics were planned out immaculately by all the law enforcement involved.

The prisoners were lead out of the jail hand cuffed and ankle shackled in pairs. Each pair was placed in a separate squad car along with two guards and a driver. Three Chippewa County cars contained the gang. The procession to Benson was led by two Swift County squads containing five armed deputies each.

The Minnesota State Highway Patrol followed the procession with two more squads containing a total of ten troopers. There was always a minimum of 26 armed officers accompanying the gangsters to court. The trip was about eighteen miles long and took about a half-hour from start to finish. This had to be a spectacular sight to see in this sleepy Minnesota countryside.

You may wonder why the tight security. This gang had a hideout in this area. As stated before, there were sympathizers and relatives that very likely would attempt a rescue. To these people, the gang was a welcome sight and heroes. They believed the gang represented an anti-establishment stance in the way that they robbed the rich. Justifying this theory was the kidnapping of an attorney and his large new car. This is just another spoonful of antisocial bologna by the gang.

After all, do you for a moment think that they just robbed the rich? Of course not; they would get drunk and take advantage of the easiest target they could find. These people were not a modem day Robin Hood and his merry men. They were vicious criminals that would hurt anyone who crossed their path. They didn't give their booty to the poor. They considered themselves the poor and kept it.

When they arrived at the court house they were paraded into a court room to face Judge Qvale. Once Judge Qvale brought the courtroom to order, the defendants were ordered to stand before the judge as he read the indictments against them. I can just imagine the pathetic look the gang was giving the judge. I'm sure they were wearing the "poor me" look on their face. I can only imagine how they really looked at this time. I don't believe any of them were walking straight and looking up with their heads held high. I think they were slumped at the shoulders and looking down at their feet. I'm sure they were worried.

All six were charged with the attempted armed robbery of Coggins Gas Station. All were charged with kidnapping Clay Johnson. Cleon, Walter, and Margaret were additionally charged with the kidnapping of J.A. (Ed) Wayne and Henry Larson. Walter was also charged with armed robbery of Coggins Gas Station on February 9, 1933. None of them were charged with attempted murder or assault with a deadly weapon. All six pled not guilty to all the charges. Not guilty?

Wait a minute. What about the confessions? All of you signed confessions. Now you plead not guilty? It took everyone by surprise. I didn't find it that surprising. They signed a confession with the hope that the court would accept a plea bargain. No bargain was agreed too or offered. They might as well go for the not guilty plea and take their chances.

Hearing the not guilty plea, Judge Qvale held the gang over for trial. He set bail at $30,000.00 for Walter, $20,000.00 for Duco and Cleon, and $5,000.00 for Blanch, Margaret, and Mabel.

It was ordered that the trial would commence April 10, 1933. The judge also found that the defendants could not afford attorneys, so he ordered a Public Defender named W. W. Merrill to represent them all.

The judge ordered the proceedings closed until motions and trial. The prisoners were taken back to Montevideo in the same manner that brought them there.

On the ride home, the realization of the seriousness of this situation set in on each and every one of them. Judge Qvale set the highest bail ever in Minnesota's history. It was evident that the court system in this county was not going to put up with this type of criminal activity at all. The system was going to set an example. All those criminals that thought Minnesota was a safe haven would need to think again. Enough was enough. Get out! Don't you dare come to this area and think for one minute that we would tolerate your presence. This gang was enough. The public got wind to the Twin Cities' secret policy on harboring criminals. They would start questioning the future employment of several high-ranking police officials and elected officials as well. The stuff was going to hit the fan and the dirt was about to land in the faces of these people.

Chippewa County was holding the Bonrud Gang and providing security and transportation, but this came at a price. Chippewa County was tallying up quite a large bill for their services. When this was all done, Swift County was going to receive a bill they may not be able to pay. The citizens of Swift County were muttering under their breath the "L" word. "Lynch them, it's cheaper!" The citizens were becoming quite hostile to the fact that the court proceedings and security was the fault of city slickers that thought they could come here and bulldoze their way through our town. Just who did they think they were messing with? We may be a poor county but one thing is for sure. You have been caught. Our poorest citizen has more character and pride than all of you put together. You should be lynched for principle and violating our values alone.

The expense of this whole ordeal could seriously hurt the county's finances. It's possible that the gang would have been lynched had it not been for Montevideo holding them in their jail. If I were them, I would be scared every time I had to go to Benson. I'm sure that some of these lynching thoughts from a very few Benson citizens made the way to the Montevideo jail and into the heads of the prisoners. This information had to trickle in from the few visitors they received. I believe the attorney kept them informed. I don't believe he was all that enthused about representing them. He was a local citizen too. He was seeing what this gang did to the community. He didn't mind at all to tell them about the thoughts of men outside these jail cells. Heck with it, scare them!

Three days before the trial was to begin the gang had a change of heart and decided to plead guilty and take their chances on sentencing. Perhaps this would also settle the citizens down as well. Was it the collective mood of the citizens that persuaded the gang to plead guilty? Justice wasn't tampered with; the thought of a stretched neck can make anyone double think. The power of suggestion was very strong. It should be said that not once did they receive any death threats from anyone. It was solely rumors and innuendoes that persuaded these people to do the right thing.

On April 10th, 1933 the prisoners were taken from Montevideo to Benson in the same fashion as before. Again there was an overkill of protection from Monte to Benson. It was a small Army of law enforcement.

When they arrived at the court house the police noticed a larger crowd than usual. The Benson police informed the other officials that most of these people were friends and relatives from Montevideo. This made all the guards extremely nervous. Were these people planning a rescue? This could be bad. This could be real bad. This could be worse than the shootout and capture.

All fears set aside, the prisoners were unloaded with armed guards surrounding them with guns drawn. They were led into the courtroom. Another very nervous moment was when the crowd followed them into the courtroom. The court room was tense. The guards were on heightened alert. They were very worried about a rescue attempt. They took a defensive stance around the prisoners. They may have been out numbered two to one but they had the advantage of weaponry fit to handle any situation.

Judge Qvale gave the court room spectators specific instructions not to interrupt the proceedings. If they choose to interrupt the courts procedures, they would be charged with contempt of court and jailed immediately. He wasn't about to let anyone spoil his court proceedings. He was in no mood to fool around with these people. I'm sure the prisoners were thinking that their friends and family were doing more harm than good. Showing up like this wasn't a show of support, it was a threat.

This whole situation with the crowd made the Judge cranky and now they weren't going to intimidate him. This was his courtroom and his trial. Get in, sit down, and shut up. The Judge ordered the proceedings to order. He ordered the prisoners to plead their case one by one in front of him. He called their names out one at a time. The prisoner would approach the bench. Their appearance was now a look of shambles. It was customary back then to wear horizontal black and white striped prison cloths. The women had the look of being dragged to court behind horses. They were dressed in stripes that weren't clean. Their hair was frizzy and uncombed. No make up or jewelry to adorn them. They were sporting thin and no sole slippers. They were hand cuffed and leg shackled. The men had their stripes on. None of them had hair cuts. The sheriff with held their shaving gear for three or four days. He thought the unshaven and un-kept men would appear indifferent to the judge. None of the prisoners had a shower for several days at a time. They had a strong odor emitting from them. Unmoved by their appearance, the Judge was methodical handing down sentences. When the individual approached his bench he would ask the same questions in the same order to each prisoner.

1. State your full name for the record.
2. What is your family history?
3. Do you understand the charges against you?
4. How do you plead? Do you plead guilty or not guilty?

All six gangsters were asked these questions and they all answered them. Most importantly they all responded *guilty* you're Honor. When the last person was questioned, the judge stated that he was ready to impose sentencing. He called the gang one by one to stand and hear his sentence.

Walter Christensen was called and he stood up to hear that he was sentenced to 5-40 years hard labor at the Stillwater State Prison

Cleon Bonrud was called and he stood up to hear he was sentenced to 5-40 years hard labor at the Stillwater State Prison.

Perley (Duco) Oliva was next to stand before the judge to hear that he was sentenced to 5-40 years hard labor at Stillwater State Prison.

Blanch Bonrud stood to hear the she was sentenced to 5 years at the Shakopee reformatory for women.

Mabel Oliva was sentenced to one year at the Shakopee reformatory for women.

Margaret Bonrud was sentenced to two years at the Shakopee reformatory for women. Her sentence was stayed. The Judge thought it would be prudent to place her in the custody of the Big Sister Institute for evaluation and treatment.

The Judge had passed sentences and now declared the proceedings closed. The prisoners were escorted back to Montevideo. What a quiet ride that must have been. The Judge threw the book at them. Only Mabel and Margaret received light sentences. Why? Why did they get off so light?

As it turns out, the Judge took mercy out on Margaret because she was only eighteen years old and she was the spark that ignited the confessions. The Judge thought she was impressionable when it came to Nobel. She was led down the wrong path and her young age wasn't mature enough to choose right from wrong. Prison would be too harsh.

Blanch received a few more years because of her involvement in aiding Cleon and Walter in kidnapping two more people during the commission of auto theft.

As far as Margaret's sentence goes it turned out the Judge didn't get this one right. Not even close. Big Sisters Institute could not reform her. She would constantly escape. With her criminal experience, little girl attitude, provocative dressing, and makeup she was able to smuggle in, her looks worked for her when she would run off with men twice her age and consort with the bad elements of society. She would drink and smoke in the dorm where it was strictly prohibited. The Big Sister admitted failure to Judge Qvale. He immediately ordered Margaret to prison and serve out her sentence. Back she went to the drab prison garb, frizzy hair and no makeup.

Mabel received a light sentence because the Judge wanted her out of prison fast so she would tend to her daughters. I don't know what the Judge was thinking at the time, but if he only would have looked into Mabel's lack of caring and nurturing, he wouldn't have given her the light sentence. For the crimes she committed in front of her daughters, she should have lost custody and thrown in the jail for twenty years. The legal system really let two children down here. This was mistake number two by this Judge. Mavis was being left alone at the apartment for weeks at a time. Darlos was being left at her Aunt Carries house in Montevideo for weeks at a time.

By all accounts from many conversations with my mother, her Uncle Fred constantly sexually molested her. Six years old and this sick man had to molest her.

If only the Judge had the insight to investigate the welfare of Mavis and Darlos. While Mabel served her time the court ordered that Mavis be placed with her Aunt Manda in Minneapolis. Darlos was placed with Carrie and the pedophile until Mabel was released. How sad. This child was abused at his will for the next year. Actually, even after Mabel's release Darlos would be staying with her aunt.

This was a bit of extra information on Mabel's sentencing. The newspapers put it best, "Woman faints as judge hands down her sentence." Yep, the drama queen struck again. The Judge saw through her and didn't even stutter as he read her sentence. The trial was over. Benson could breathe again. The escorts relaxed.

The only thing left to do was to keep these prisoners housed and fed until the State could arrange transportation that would deliver them to prison.

They had been model prisoners through this whole ordeal. The Sheriff thought he would reward them by allowing visitors to see them before they were paraded off to prison.

After a couple days of visitors seeing the prisoners, the Sheriff started having second thoughts about his generosity. At least fifty people visited the first day and the second day looked like there may be more. Where did all these people come from? The Sheriff put the visitation to a halt. He just admitted to the prisoners that there were just too many people to keep track of.

The Sheriff spent a lot of time with Cleon. Cleon was a very likeable guy. The Sheriff would enter his cell many times for a chat. They would sometimes talk for hours. The Sheriff really liked him and unknowingly let his guard down a bit. One afternoon he entered Cleon's cell to have another little chat with him. As the Sheriff entered the cell, a shinny object caught his eye partially exposed from under the mattress. The Sheriff has seen things like this before. He pulled out his gun and trained it on Cleon. He told Cleon to back up to the wall and freeze. Cleon was on the other side of a threat backed up with a gun and he complied with the Sheriffs order. The Sheriff reached under the mattress and pulled out several hack saw blades and a key carved from wood. The Sheriff back out of the cell and locked it behind him. He counted twelve hacksaw blades. The key was nearly finished and trying the key in the cell door proved that Cleon was close to escaping, perhaps within a day. He expressed his disappointment in Cleon and returned to his office.

The Sheriff picked up the phone and called the Highway Patrol. They are responsible for providing the transportation for the prisoners. The Sheriff told the State Patrol that he "wanted these people out now! Come and get them!" They were now more than he could handle.

The Highway Patrol took this call seriously. They heard panic and nervousness in the Sheriffs voice. The Highway Patrol immediately put together a convoy to retrieve the prisoners and transport them to Stillwater. A couple hours later the convoy of Highway Patrol men arrived at the Sheriffs office. The exchange of paperwork and the transferring of the prisoners took less than fifteen minutes. The prisoners were hand cuffed and ankle shackled and marched out to the vehicles. Once they were loaded in the cars, the lawmen said their good buy's and the convoy left Monte destination Stillwater State Prison. Sheriff Nels Peterson was glad the gang was gone. No telling what would have happened in a few days. He thought the fanners in Benson would nab the gang and lynch them, or their relatives around Montevideo would attempt a rescue. Either way, the threats were now gone. Now it was back to the routine and mundane every day duties. Arresting drunks and calming family squabbles.

The gang was on their way to prison. Cleon and Walter already had a good idea on what to expect. They have done time before. They were imprisoned at the St. Cloud Reformatory. This old prison was a very imposing sight that sits on the fringe of St. Cloud, Minnesota. The stone walls are tall and gray. On the top are layers of barbed wire and guard stations every 100 feet or so. Cleon and Walter thought St. Cloud was imposing and cold. Well, I'm here to tell you, St. Cloud Reformatory looks like a Life Magazine Blue Ribbon Show Case Prison compared to Stillwater State Prison. This prison has an attitude, a very mean attitude. It's cold in the winter and unbearably hot in the summer. It's a huge factory that produces all sorts of consumer goods, including license plates. It's an ugly place to spend any time at all, and each of the gangsters was going to spend a lot of time here.

The girls were on their way to a similar situation. Even though their sentences were lighter, it still didn't make life any easier. Oh well. It was our way for payback. We the people make laws and rules.

If you break the law, sympathy goes out the window. It's off to a dark, cold and imposing prison.

You're not going to live in hotel like conditions. If that were the case, everyone would want to go to prison.

With the exception of Margaret and Blanch, the Bonrud gang stayed fairly close. Walter was treated like a brother. Cleon and Margaret divorced while serving time. Margaret and Blanch just disappeared from the scene. After the divorce, they never heard from them again.

Walter was released on parole in May, 1940. He was given his release June 28, 1945. Of all the gang members, Walter spent the most time in prison. He stayed away from the Bonrud's while on parole. He liked his freedom more than his old friendships.

Cleon was paroled on May 29, 1939. He was totally released on May 14, 1941. His parole was uneventful and clean of crimes. I wouldn't swear to it, but I think that Walter and Cleon remained friends even after their release.

Duco was paroled May 29, 1939 and went to work for his old boss, John Christenson. John took Duco under his employ long before he met that corrupted old nag Mabel. John swore to the parole board that if it wasn't for her, Duco would have remained lawful. John owned an electrical contracting business. Duco went through his apprenticeship with big John. He became a journeyman with the help and guidance from John.

It was John's guarantee to the parole board to keep Duco employed. He had one problem though. He mentioned to the parole board that it was his opinion that Mabel was an extreme bad influence on Duco.

He said that they should divorce and never see each other again. The parole board took this under advisement.

My parents knew John Christenson. They became family friends. John even sent a wedding gift to my parents on their wedding day. For many years, my dad was under the impression that big John was Duco's parole officer. I corrected him a few years back. I told him that John was once Duco's employer. I informed Dad that by the time he was introduced to Duco, in 1946, Duco already was completely released. Duco was completely released from custody May 14th, 1941. My dad didn't believe me until I showed him the Governor's Release and restored civil rites. I asked my dad one poignant question, "Do you think Duco would ever be friends with any type of law enforcement official?" Duco hated any law enforcement official.

My Great Uncle Cleon was a dapper type of guy. He was always dressed to the nines. He had a great attitude with a flash of class. He was smooth and very good looking. He enjoyed the underbelly of Minneapolis. He loved the strip clubs and they loved him. Cleon would have a different exotic dancer on his arm every other day and night. He liked the wild side. He received his total release in 1940. He served in the Army during WWII and left with an honorable discharge.

One night on his way to Minneapolis from Montevideo, he fell to sleep behind the wheel near Excelsior, Minnesota on Highway 7. He hit a huge Oak tree. I don't think Oaks get any bigger than this one. He hit it at approximately 70 MPH. I think he broke every bone in his body. How he lived through this was a mystery to all his attending doctors and family. He was in a cast from his head to his feet. Yes, he had a cast on his head as well. He looked like the mummy. This certainty didn't dampen his spirits. He just wanted to get back to the bars and girls. He continued his fast paced life for a couple more years. One night he got into a car with a drunk driver. They went speeding through the streets of Minneapolis until a semi truck crossed the street directly in front of them. They were going to fast for the breaks to stop them. They went under the trailer. Both men were decapitated.

Duco spent six years in prison and by all accounts, he was a model prisoner. He made friends easily and he treated the guards with respect. He was always clean-shaven and his clothes were cleaned and pressed.

After his conviction he was court ordered to surrender 75% of his earnings to his former wife June. She was raising their two children. In prison he was earning about $30.00 to $40.00 a month. That meant June was receiving about $30.00 a month from Duco. Mabel was furious over this financial arrangement. When she was released, she too demanded part of Duco's salary for help in supporting Mavis and Darlos.

The warden agreed with Mabel. The money that was being deducted from Duco's monthly salary would be split in to two. Now June would get half of what she was getting before.

The Warden, Parole Board, prison guards and friends thought it would be best if Duco would forget about Mabel. Even in a men's prison Mabel's reputation preceded her. She had a bad reputation. Everyone told Duco to drop her. He could do better. He could attract a better woman than her. John Christenson was even on that bandwagon. Nobody expected him to return to June, but there are a lot of nicer women out there. Duco would appease these conversations by agreeing with the critics.

Mabel spent her time in prison uneventful. She was a loner and didn't make any friends. She didn't think she belonged there. She looked down her nose at ever inmate as if to say, "You deserve to be here, not me."

Her attitude rubbed the guards the wrong way. They always came up with sewing jobs that were beneath her. She repaired petticoats, socks and underwear. Occasionally she would be allowed to sew a dress for her daughters. Years later Mabel asked the girls how the dresses were holding up. The two girls knew of just one. That was a cruel cut against Mabel. The guards never did send the dresses out to the girls. Heck, they kept them for their daughters. This hardened Mabel even more. If she wasn't a bitter and spiteful woman before, she was now.

Mabel spent her time in the reformatory and was released in late 1934. After her release you would think that a mother would want to reunite with her children immediately. Not Mabel. She wrote a letter to the Warden at Stillwater State Prison stating that she would be released in a couple days. She requested that additional time of one half hour be granted to her and Duco upon her arrival. It was Stillwater Prison and Duco that would be her first stop.

She needed to make a few points clear with her husband and the Warden. First and foremost she demanded that June's spousal support be stopped because she remarried. She figured that June's new husband could support his newfound family. She also wanted half the child support. Mabel figured that her two children qualified for care from Duco. The other point being, no more visits from June, period: "He was my husband, not hers".

The Warden didn't take her attitude kindly. He understood her point of view, but the attitude had to go. He mentioned that he didn't care for the way she came across in his prison. He made it clear that this attitude wouldn't be tolerated in this facility and if she continued with her bad temperament, she would be banned from visiting anyone here. On the other hand, he did promise to take the child support issue under advisement and report his findings to her shortly.

Mabel wasn't accustomed to a man talking to her like that. She stood up, huffed and left the prison. I don't think Duco got a word in at all. At least nothing was mentioned in the transcripts.

A few days later the warden issued his decision to Mabel and June. His decision was backed by opinions from state attorneys. The warden agreed that June should not visit Duco in prison and he ordered her banned from the building. Spousal support would be split two ways. All child support will remain with June and her children. These children belonged to Duco directly. Mabel's two children were step children and would not qualify for support under the rule of the day. Mabel was advised to seek support from the fathers of the two girls.

It should be mentioned that after her release from prison, Mabel made at least one trip to Stillwater Prison a week. She would also visit her brother Cleon and her friend Walter. She remained loyal to the gang.

Mabel and money, it was an evil relationship. She would do anything for money. Before she met Duco and during her final days with her husband Julian Peterson, she took up the oldest profession in the world. At the time of her divorce from Julian, they had a daughter Mavis. It would be a 6 years before Darlos came along. Julian was long gone by then.

GRANDMA AND GRANDPA

I knew Cleon somewhat. He was a person that just down right struck a resemblance to Clark Gable. He was a smooth operator and a very handsome fellow. He always dressed up with a tie, and coat, shined shoes and a Clark Gable moustache. His hair was dark and every hair on his head had its place. His voice and manner of speaking was always soft. He had a great sense of humor and he also had a different exotic dancer on his arm every time I saw him. I was a pimpled face teenager at the time when he started bringing girlfriends around to Duco's river lot. If they looked at me and gave me a wink, and they usually did, I would just turn into a puddle of goop. I think Cleon put them up to that. These girls were just gorgeous. One time one of these girls kissed me on the cheek. I was beside myself for a week. It's really too bad that Cleon was killed in a car accident. I was looking forward to hanging around with Cleon His life was so intriguing. Well that didn't happen, instead I had my wild times in Germany serving in the Army. I look back at Cleon today and I can understand how the rest of the gang came together. Cleon was a soft spoken persuasive man. He knew where the action was and he knew how to work with people. I liked Cleon when I was young. I didn't know anyone who didn't like him.

I really can't comment on Walter. I never met him. I heard Duco and Cleon talk about a Walter, but at the time the name meant nothing to me. Blanch and Margaret just disappeared. When they got out of prison they vanished never to be heard from again. Cleon and Blanch divorced while in prison. Those women may have stayed in the Minneapolis area, or they may have moved out of state. Cleon, Walter, Duco or Mabel never spoke of them again.

For me, that just leaves Duco and Mabel. Now I can talk about those two. I was twenty years old when I found out about them. Prior to my joining the Army in 1966, I had a true love/hate relationship with them. Duco was the one I was on guard about the most. He was the meanest ~~son of a bitch~~ I ever knew. The guy was pure mean. Not so much with adults, or anyone that was bigger than him, and with him being a husky 6 feet man there were few of them, so that just left kids. I really believe he hated kids and especially me.

Duco was born December 30th, 1901 in Hutchinson, Minnesota. He was raised on a farm with an older brother and a younger brother. He performed chores without question or complaint. By all accounts, he had an exceptional childhood. He was one of the few children at the time to graduate from school.

Electricity was making its way out into the country. Duco saw opportunity here in the electrical field. Duco was a bright man to say the least. He moved to Minneapolis in 1920 to take up being an apprentice in the electrical construction area with John Christenson's electrical contracting business. John liked Duco's work ethics. His schooling and training came easy for him. He was quite proficient at wiring houses and factories. He was a quick learner and a tireless worker. Duco dated and married his first wife June in 1921. They had two children together. A girl and a boy made for a perfect life.

Duco was a very good provider. His family had a nice roof over their head, food on the table, money to spend, and a good sense of stability. Sounds like the perfect family to me. That was until I read a report from his divorce proceedings. He liked beer; lots and lots of beer. When he would go out on a binge he wouldn't return for a couple days. After being out drinking beer and chasing women for a couple days without any sleep, he would turn vicious against June and the kids.

June didn't put up with this from him very long. In 1929, she filled for divorce, claiming adultery and indifference toward the family. There wasn't much of a fight from Duco; he was now quite comfortable with a new girl on his arm, Mabel Bonrud. The divorce was finalized in 1930. This, however, was not the end of June vs. Duco and Mabel.

From what I saw in the relationship between Duco and Mabel, I just don't know what he was thinking. Mabel was married and divorced and she had a profession that would normally turn a man off. She was a prostitute. My earliest memory of the two of them was when they owned an apartment building in south Minneapolis. It has 4 units and a garage that Duco kept his Cadillac parked in. I might have been five years old and I remember that building and I also remember the arguments those two had. They were ferocious.

During his parole hearings they were stuck with each other in a love and hate relationship. It was known to them that John and the parole board did not like their union. They constantly warned Duco that his parole could be delayed unless he denounced his marriage to Mabel. Duco and Mabel lied to officials and his employer John Christenson about the relationship. The lie they told was that they would not see each other and come to terms about their romantic feelings. They claimed that the romantic feelings were fading. For them to stay together they had to lie. When Duco was going through the parole interviews John Christenson was making it hard on Duco to see Mabel at all.

John was not only Duco's employer; he down right took Duco under his protection and stood up for Duco at the parole hearings. John Christenson attended every parole hearing guaranteeing the board that he would gladly hire the hard working Duco. After a few of these meetings in which Duco was turned down because of the severity of the crime, John got to know and understand Mabel better. The more he knew her, the more he disliked her. He went as far as to write the parole board a letter maintaining his desire to hire Duco, but he mentioned that it would be in Duco's best interest to sever his relationship with Mabel and then divorce her.

He claimed that Mabel has been a bad influence on Duco, and she alone led him down the path of crime.

This letter was read to Duco at his next parole hearing. When asked what he was thinking, Duco paused for a few moments and then said, "John was my employer before I got in trouble, and he's sticking by me even now. How could I possibly ignore his advice?"

This was what the board wanted to hear. They recommended parole under the condition that he would stay away from Mabel. The other standard provisions were also agreed to by Duco. No weapons, alcohol, no loans for cars or houses, no patronizing saloons where alcohol is served and no contact with known criminals. In a couple days he was released on parole.

After his release, Duco set himself up real nice in a one room apartment. He worked hard and he totaled a lot of over time. He was making some darn good cash. He purchased new furniture and appliances, and even bought a car. Parole life was good for him. His parole officer gave him very high marks.

At first Duco and Mabel agreed to stay apart for a while, at least until Duco can have a history of good behavior with his parole officer. Just as things were going Duco's way, Mabel did show up again, earlier than planned. It's very obvious that most of their thinking was from below the belt. Ignoring all the advice from John Christenson and the parole board, they decided to get back together.

When John Christensen got wind of this reunion he rushed over to Duco's parole officer office building. They discussed the situation that Duco was putting him self into. The parole officer had an ace up his sleeve. He asked John to accompany him to Duco's apartment. It was fortunate that Duco was home alone.

The parole officer and John both expressed their concerns about the reunion. They both told Duco that he would be better off if he divorced her and never see her again. Duco tried to convince them that Mabel has changed her ways and was becoming a good citizen again plus a better wife.

This was where the parole officer pulls the ace out of his sleeve. He said to Duco, "Look my friend. I have investigated your loving Mabel Oliva and while you were being so naive about her love for you, an Arnold Christenson, (no relations to any Christenson's mentioned before) has been shacking up with her." Duco turned white as a ghost. He put his head in his hands and slowly rocked himself back and forth. After a bit of silence, he looked up and admitted that they were right all along and he would divorce Mabel.

The two men left Duco with his thoughts and drove back to the parole officers' office.

They were satisfied that Duco was now convinced that Mabel wasn't for him.

On June 10ᵗh, 1939, Duco called John Christensen and told him he was concerned for Mabel's welfare. John was confused and then asked, "What was going on?"

The Arnold Christensen that was living with her had gone nuts over a conversation about Duco. It seems that all conversations were about Duco and Arnold had enough. He pulled out a gun and threatened to shoot Mabel if she didn't quit talking about Duco.

Somehow Mabel broke away from Arnold and called Duco. He in turn called the police. When the police arrived Arnold was on top of Mabel beating ~~the hell out~~ her. They dragged him off from her and took him off to jail. He was charged with carrying a concealed weapon, a .45 caliber pistol. That was the end of that relationship.

This incident put Duco into a higher state of admiration for Mabel. They began their relationship as husband and wife again. At first it was secretive, but after a while Duco would have a heart-to-heart talk with his parole officer. He would explain that they were truly in love and they want to get back together again as a wedded couple.

For some reason the parole officer had a change of mind about the two of them. Perhaps he figured they deserve each other. Perhaps he figured out that a legally wedded couple can't be forced not to see each other by a parole agent or committee. . He not only gave Duco the thumbs up, he also recommended his unconditional release from prison and parole. Duco did prove that he can be a citizen that stays on the right side of the law; he also proved to his parole agent that he could be a pain ~~in the ass~~. The agent couldn't send Duco back to prison for being with his wife, plus he was tired of putting up with Duco's border line antics. On May 29, 1941 Duco received his unconditional release from his prison sentence signed by the governor. He was a free man again with all his civil rights restored. He could vote again. He could also have a mortgage, and a car loan. Drink booze and beer, consort with known criminals and own a gun. He exercised all his rights. He would also live in a lie he created about Mabel. He couldn't get rid of her now. Living full time with such a woman has again corrupted Duco. His mindset changed. Duco and Mabel would often get into fights involving fists and knives. His drinking was everyday now. He would get delirious when drunk and go after Darlos. He would look up all his prison buddies and have them over for drinks. After a belly full of beer and the brain soaked in alcohol he would in turn slap Mabel silly. She would go at his throat with a knife when he slept. What a loving and tender relationship.

Mabel was born in Baxter, Minnesota on July 27, 1902 into a family of thirteen brothers and sisters. Two of her siblings passed away in childhood and Mabel's' parents passed away when she was a teenager. Mabel was the forth from the youngest.

When she turned fifteen, she moved from Baxter to Watson, Minnesota. It didn't take long to build a reputation in that little town so after a year passed she moved to Montevideo, Minnesota.

In 1920, she married Julian Peterson and they had a daughter, Mavis. They lived in Montevideo for a period of time when all of a sudden Mabel got itchy feet and filed for divorce June 25, 1925 with Judge Harold Baker. Her divorce trial was conducted in Renville County. The divorce decree was finalized August 12, 1929.

Julian visited my mother in the mid 1970's at her home in Lakeville, Minnesota. I was able to meet the man and I found him to be a very nice fellow with good manners and appearance. I'll say that he was also nervous, who could blame him?. I guess when I think about it, the poor guy came to a person's house to visit a person that he really didn't know.

The conversation mother had with Julian confirmed Mabel's feelings toward her in that Mabel always referred to her as, "the unwanted one". Darlos told Julian that she was led to believe that Julian had offered Mabel his name to make Darlos appear legitimate. Darlos thanked him for allowing her to have his name. Julian had to stop her to say to her disbelief that he was not her step father, nor did he give Mabel permission to use him as the father on the birth certificate. Julian confirmed that my mother was born from a person that was one of Mabel's steady customers. He did not know his name. He also stated that he and not Mabel filed for the divorce. He said that it became apparent that Mabel was slipping back into her evil ways. She was staying out nights drinking and flirting with other men. On occasion she would prostitute herself for extra money. Julian said he would not tolerate this behavior any more, so he divorced her. My dad and mother sincerely thanked him for clearing up some issues. Deep down in my mothers sole she thought that he would admit that he was her father. Mathematically, it wasn't possible but she was in denial of the time table.

I give the fellow a ton of credit for showing up like he did. I think in a way he got even with Mabel. I'm sure that she was a thorn in his side for years. By telling Darlos the truth, he knew that that my mother would see her mother and read her the riot act. It was at this time when my dislike for Mabel escalated from just disliking her to hatred. Mabel lived a lie and spread it to her daughter, the unwanted one.

Now back to the 1930's. Mabel always relied on a husband's income. To prove her stupidity, she forgot to ask for child support in divorce court. Without Julian's income she found it hard to stay in Montevideo. Montevideo wasn't showing any promise of a job or a husband. Like in Baxter, she had developed a bad girl reputation. She had enough of this place so she packed up and moved to Minneapolis. She would be in for a little surprise when she hit Minneapolis. Cleon was there, her favorite party animal. When they hooked up Cleon told her what a great time he was having in Minneapolis. He was out nearly every night dancing and drinking. Mabel couldn't wait to party with her younger brother. Off they went to the good life.

Well, it didn't take long to figure out that these good times cost big bucks. She was broke.

Now what? She doesn't have a job, other than washing dishes a couple hours a day at a local cafe. She wondered how Cleon always had money. She never saw him go to a job. She didn't know it at the time, but Cleon was a gangster. He robbed people for a living.

Another Bonrud prone to crime was another younger brother named Nobel. Nobel was living in Watertown, South Dakota. Nobel was pulling off a robbery about the same time Cleon was pulling a scam in Minneapolis. Nobel got caught and because of his age he wasn't prosecuted for his crime. There are no court records in South Dakota showing any criminal court convictions against Nobel. He was a rebel to be sure, but he was clean in the eyes of the law.

Cleon on the other hand was caught and convicted on larceny charges Cleon would be serving time at the St. Cloud State Reformatory.

This is an ugly looking prison. It sits on the out skirts of St. Cloud, Minnesota. It's made with tall gray and tan stone that can give you the shivers to look at. They are very tall and thick. The last time I saw the prison there was barbed wire on top of the wall and guard towers manned with armed guards. It was here that Cleon struck up a friendship with Walter Christenson. They would get together after their respective release from the St. Cloud Prison. They stayed together and formed a mini gang that operated in Minnesota and northern Iowa. They managed to avoid the police investigations by committing crimes outside the immediate Twin Cities area. Nobel also made his way to Minneapolis and joined his brother and also participated in the criminal activities.. The Bonrud gang was taking shape.

Prior to Cleon being released from prison, Mabel was coming apart in Monte. She was at a loss for friendship and she was also at a loss for steady work. She would work several cafe jobs in a day and receive peanuts for wages. She was constantly late with her rent and she would be kicked out a soon as the first months rent was over due. Darlos remembers moving from apartment to apartment constantly. Mabel had the thought that Minneapolis employers would be a bit more forgiving for a person with an 8th grade education. As it turned out, Minneapolis businesses were over loaded with people looking for work and those who were standing in line for a job had higher education credentials.

Mabel was now broken in spirit. Big town party girl was begging for money in the street.

She had failed miserably. Cleon was in prison and couldn't give her any advice. She was so low that she had to look up to see bottom.

She decided to turn to prostitution. It was all she had left. As it turned out, even being a prostitute didn't bring in an income. Not only was she not good at selling herself, the Depression took money away from the men that would normally use prostitutes. Times were hard.

During 1926, Mabel was into criminal activity. Sometimes she would give herself to a man free. She would pull the right strings and push the right buttons and then like magic, she would be moving in with the guy. Now all she had to do was screw the guy for room and board. The guy eventually figured he was getting screwed in more ways than one. Things in his home would start disappearing. Mabel just couldn't get it right. These guys would find out the truth about her motives and then beat the hell out of her as they bounced her towards the door.

If she would have just settled down with one of the many guys she moved in with, who knows, maybe she could have found security. But no, not Mabel, not only did she steal property, she would leave for days on end and practice her layaway plan on all sorts of different men. She would seek out the ones that would share their bottle of booze.

Now the guy she left behind was getting real steamed when she stayed away. He was stuck babysitting Mavis. When Mabel sobered up she would return to a beating and a kick in the moneymaker out the door. Then she would start all over again. This is a true vicious circle.

Mabel did this act for a few years. About the time that Mavis would settle down to a new home, her mother would screw it up and they would have to move again. Mabel eventually wised up and sent Mavis to live with her sister Manda in Wisconsin. Now Mabel had a bit more freedom to work herself and find men that would take her in. The word faithful has never entered her mind.

In 1926, one of her customers got her pregnant. On January 17, 1927 Darlos was born. This was truly not good for Mabel. Having this baby really cramped her style. She refused to settle down and raise another child. Darlos was the "unwanted one".

Mabel listed Julian Peterson as the father. I don't believe she meant to give Darlos legitimacy, I believe the legitimacy was meant for her. She needed a name to tell her family. They would swallow that Julian was the father. Mabel would make up some kind of story to have her cleared of prostitution in her families' eyes.

Mabel would often hitch hike to Montevideo. Now she had a baby in tow, Darlos. Mabel was going to give her sister Carrie a con job. She would make it so Carrie would beg keep Darlos at her house.

When she arrived in Montevideo and visited with her sister Carrie and her husband Fred her plan was falling into place. Carrie was falling in love with baby Darlos. The plan worked. Mabel left Montevideo without Darlos. Carrie didn't know it at the time but she would become the care taker for Darlos on a near full time basis for many years to come.

As years passed by, Mabel occasionally traveled back to Montevideo to see Carrie and Darlos. It wasn't surprising that Carrie figured out what Mabel did, but when it came right down to it, they enjoyed having her.

As Darlos grew into her teen years, she began to question her mother about Julian. Darlos put two and two together and she figured out that there was no way that Julian could be her father. Every time Darlos questioned Mabel, a different answer would spew from her lying mouth.

Darlos had another serious problem that she thought her mother should know. She told Mabel that her Uncle Fred was molesting her, on a regular basis. He has been doing that for years now. He's been touching her in places and telling her how pretty she was.

Mabel went ballistic. Not against her brother in law, she unloaded on her daughter. "What are you doing to invite him like that? It's your fault. If you flirt with him, then you have it coming. Now behave yourself."

By the time Darlos was in her twenties, her mind was so twisted by what happened to her at the hands of Fred and the lies her mother told her about her father, and the dirty things that happened to her when she was with her mother when she entertained customers in the same bed at the same time she took naps as a toddler; she needed mental health care and hospitalization. In all, I remember my mother receiving shock treatments on three different occasions. Even these treatments couldn't erase the evil treatment she was subjected too as a child. She could never get her abused childhood out of her mind.

Going back to the 1930's, somehow or another Mabel finally struck it rich. She met Duco. At first it was a normal boy meets girl thing. They courted for a while and then they were married in Hudson, Wisconsin in 1932. Mabel finally found the security she had been looking for. Duco was a mature, hard-working electrician. He was making $200.00 a month and that was big dollars back then. They were meant for each other. He made good money, and Mabel could spend it, and all she had to do was give him sex and booze.

Duco had just gone through a divorce. He was beat up bad in court by his ex-wife June. He would be paying child support for his two children and also spousal support to June.

Meeting and marrying Mabel was refreshing for him. They would drink themselves into stupors and have sex all night long. They were totally made to be with each other. Duco had no problem taking in the two girls. He made enough money to support both families.

By now Cleon and Nobel had been out of prison for a few months. They teamed up with another prison cellmate Walter Christenson. He was another two bit hoodlum. The three of them became fast friends. They also became a gang. In late 1931, they started their escapades of robberies and kidnappings. They were being smart about their crimes. They would pick an area in southern Minnesota and northern Iowa; hit it with all they have, and then leave the area and never to return. It was working great for them.

In the mean time, the Perley H Oliva (Duco, Duke) family was getting kind of bored doing the same thing day in and day out. Get up in the morning, go to work. Come home to dinner and booze and then tumble in the sheets for a couple hours. They needed some entertainment. Mabel had just the fellows that could help them in that area, Cleon.

Now Cleon had a couple others that also enjoyed a good time. Cleon and his wife Blanch, Nobel and his young bride Margaret, and their trusty old friend Walter have formed a gang. Duco and Mabel would hook up with them. This was the beginning of a beautiful relationship. The Bonrud Gang has been formed.

By now Duco was paying for an apartment at 1211 Franklin Avenue. The gang would party there night after night. Every Friday and Saturday night they would fill up a couple flasks full with booze and head of to the dance hall. They would dance the night away until the place closed. Then it's back to the apartment for more drinking. Duco just ate this life style up. It was great. In the morning the apartment looked like a war zone. Bodies scattered everywhere, ashtrays overflowing, booze bottles everywhere, and the smell of puke from someone. If the two girls were home, it was there duty to make coffee and breakfast for those who could stomach it.

About now I imagine the scenario for starting a crime spree would simply start with perhaps Duco saying, "Gees, the girls, let's take Mavis to Manda's for a short time, and then let's take Darlos back to Montevideo." Everyone agreed. When the two girls are gone, we can really party.

This time it would be a different trip to Montevideo. After dropping Mavis off at Manda's, Duco went back to the apartment to get Darlos and the rest of the gang. When he went into the apartment Cleon walked up next to Duco and put his arm around his shoulder and said, "We talked something over with Mabel that we need to mention to you." Cleon went on to explain what the boys have been up to and gave Mabel and Duco an invitation to join in on their sprees of adventure.

Duco couldn't resist. Of course he would join up with them. The Bonrud gang roster was full. On their way to Montevideo with Darlos in the car, the whole gang got the bug to rob a store, and that's just what they did. It was Duco's second time that he broke the law. The first time it was a liquor violation with a ten-dollar fine. This time if he got caught, the fine would be greater. It would be prison.

That Sunday night on February 26, 1933 the Bonrud gang couldn't avoid the end result of their chosen activity. They have been fueling their brains with alcohol for a few days and judging by my life's drinking experiences, drinking that many days in a row will for sure qualify a person as a binge drinker or perhaps an alcoholic. That much drinking in that amount of time suppresses the appetite and the alcohol takes a bigger toll on the thought process. Even before they nabbed Mr. Johnson they were so stupefied they were bound to slip up and get caught. They were so drunk Cleon and Walter couldn't figure out how to operate the new Buick. How much different could the Buicks operation be? I'm sure it's still gas, clutch, shift the gears, and brake.

When they were involved in the shoot out they still had to be wasted. It's apparent that at the very least all the men were firing pistols. Not being there I believe at least one of the girls also fired at Oscar that night. Oscar fired nine shots as stated in the Coroners Inquest. There was no testimony as to how many shots were fired at Oscar. I think that there were at least 4 of the gang members firing at Oscar. I assume each had a 6 bullet capacity pistol. There were statements made that the gangs guns were revolvers but the caliber is unknown. Figuring how many shots the gang fired I would lean to a light calculation and say maybe just two guns had to be reloaded and the other two maybe fired less than 5 shots. Pure speculation adds up to 18 – 24 shots taken at Oscar. Even if you think that number is too high, cut it in half. It's equal to or exceeding the number of shops fired by Oscar. That is still a lot of bullets. It only takes one to hit its target. The second and final intentional pass at Oscar is the strangest. On the previous run, Oscar opened fire from across the street. This took the gang by total surprise. On the final pass the gang fired everyplace except where Oscar was. They fired at the station and Oscar was still across the street.

After the shooting and fast forwarding to roaming the country side with the kidnapped victim Henry Larson, I believe the gang was still totally drunk. They couldn't remember where they left the shot up Buick and their comrades. More evident was the fact that they grew up in this area yet they were lost.

The gang was destined to get caught. It was a good thing they did get caught. It's quite evident they would eventually seriously hurt someone or even kill someone. They carried this hold up adventure to far. They stuck their necks out one too many times and the law grabbed it and wrung it out.

THEY'RE ALL GONE NOW

Years passed by until Darlos met Jack Halverson and they married in 1946. This somewhat stabilized Darlos by having a good provider. Jack was a hard worker. He would eventually go to Dunwoody Trade School and take up heating and air conditioning through the schools sheet metal classes. He joined the union and enjoyed employment for many years until his retirement.

They would have four children, one boy and 3 younger girls. I'm that boy. I grew up not caring for Mabel and Duco. They always would express a lack of positive emotion towards me and I felt that all the way into my formative years. Once I grew to the age of 7, I became a little slave to their needs. I never wanted to spend any time at their home. When I did spend time, Duco would always have a list of chores for me. These chores were sometimes beyond my skills. They also were designed to last all day until Duco would arrive home from work. He would then drink 8 – 10 bottles of beer and get cranky. He would come up with more chores to carry me to bedtime. I can't recall ever just playing when I was with them. Mabel would guard me like a prison guard. If I didn't perform the chores, into a locked closet I would go. There were worse episodes but that will be for another time.

Duco died in February 1970 from cancer of the pancreas. It was painful for him. He was allowed to die at home. I went to visit him a few times a month and even with me being a young adult fresh from military service, he still had to have complete control over me. Living in an apartment building and he didn't have a garage for his Cadillac. When I visited him he would have me wash his car. Like a complete fool, I would drive it to a car wash and at my expense, have it cleaned. Why he wanted washed so often, (once a week), is beyond me. He no longer could drive.

The weeks I didn't wash it, one of his neighbors would wash it. This person would eventually buy the car from Mabel. As I remember, she received $1500.00 for a 1969 Fleetwood.

The night he died my mother and grandmother were at his bedside. Mother said he struggled a lot during the process, but he remained unconscious through it.

His funeral turned out to have a very large crowd. My dad and I could only speculate who some of the people were. We never knew these people and assumed they were from the old days.

Mavis died in November 1974. She had a cancer in her blood that couldn't be controlled back then. My aunt Mavis was the kindest and most gentle person on this Earth. Her death was painful to all that knew her.

Mabel gave me a hard time prior to her death June 24, 1991. After Duco died she went through the money they accumulated in just a few short years. The money she received was from the sale of their house on Portland Ave. and the Mille Lac lake property. The Portland sale was a balloon payment from a contract for deed sale. She squandered the money on trips to Los Vegas, furniture and she gave a lot of it away. Over a couple years she spent well over $35,000.00 with nothing to show for it. She did the same thing when she was in her prime of life back in the 1920's and 1930's. She just could not manage money.

Eventually my mother and I had to take over her finances. Mabel signed over power of attorney to us. The first thing we did was to call her creditors and tell them she was broke and couldn't fulfill payback obligations. They had no choice but to quit billing her. She had nothing. If her credit rating got bad, so what, I cut up her cards. She didn't need credit now. She would be going on assisted living.

We moved her out of her apartment and put her into a county financial assisted high rise building. Being as broke as she was, the rent was minimal. We controlled every aspect of her finances to include her grocery shopping, liquor store purchases, and hair dresser appointments. She liked the fact that we took the burden of finance off her shoulders. We gave her a small cash allowance once a week for her to spend on anything she wanted. That's more than she ever gave me when I did all those chores at her house.

Eventually she started leaving the bathtub water running over in the bathroom and leaving the stove on. If she was cooking food, it would burn and set off the fire alarms. This was happening a couple times a week. The building supervisors advised us to place her into a nursing home. We also got the same opinion from her doctor. Mabel hated the thought of being in a home. We put her into a home close to where we lived.

Mabel wanted a farewell party in her apartment. We had no problem with that, so we helped her organize the party. We had some of her apartment friends and relatives attend.

On the night of her party people brought gifts. She was having fun opening them and if it was from a resident she would moan her discontent of her leaving. Of coarse there were a few tears from her and some residents. A lot of this was actually the drama queen coming out again.

My wife and I also brought a gift. It was signed from us and our young son. When she picked it up to open she noticed that it was from us. She wound up and threw it at us and said, "I don't want anything from you Halverson's ever again!" This really upset my wife. She grabbed our son a left. She was hot! Who could blame her? This wasn't her fight. I knew this is the way grandma can get to me. She's a dirty fighter. I was so stunned I couldn't react. I just stood there and stared at the old witch. After a moment I regained my composure. I turned around and went after my wife. I caught up to her in the buildings visitors lobby. She was crying, of coarse, and stated that she would never see her again. At about the same time my parents and sisters arrived in the lobby and expressed their support for me and my family. Now I couldn't wait to get her into the home with the wishes she lives a long time.

From that point on Mabel and I had a very guarded relationship. I have never liked her and the feeling was vise versa. The day came to move her into the home. I made her ride with me. I wanted the tension so tight between us that it would be a visible aura around us. My whole life with her was full of the same type of actions she expressed at that party. She was just mean.

Once in the home she tried to be cordial with her room mate. It never worked though. As stated before, she didn't make friends easy. She didn't know how to be cordial. She just knew how to be mean and to bully her way through life's problems. The nurses told us that they would work on that skill while she stayed here. To a small degree they helped. She finally had a room mate that would listen to her. Actually, this room mate was a spy for the nurses. Her job was to report any odd behavior from Mabel. Then the nurses would use that intelligence and apply it to a learning curve for Mabel.

Shortly before her death I stopped by to visit her. I brought her favorite snack, beer and sardines. Her room mate hated that snack. It gave Mabel horrible gas attacks that nearly drove the room mate out of the room. During one of these visits I asked her why she wouldn't tell my mother who her father is. I guess this wasn't any of my business because her statement to me was, "I hate you! I know some people that will take care of you and then make it so nobody ever finds your body!"

"What! Grandma, do you know what you just said?" her reply was, "You heard me, they'll never find your body!" Good grief, is she delusional or just that full of hate against me? I think both.

I didn't hang around. I knew what she said could never be fulfilled. All her cronies are dead. What would make her say something like that? I wasn't worried about my well being, what bothered me was the statement. How could murder formulate in her mind like that? From then on I have had the notion that the gang may have committed the most vicious, ultimate crime. I took notice that Passholt visited Duco a few times in prison.

Was Passholt trying to find another weak link in Duco? Could the investigators have closed their case too soon? Did the quick confessions have an alternative purpose? Confessing may have drawn the investigators away from some unsolved murders. Is that possible? Did that gang kill someone? They certainly had the mindset for it. Behavior by the gang speaks for its self. They tried to kill the Chief of Police in Benson. They tried to kill him with three salvos of gun fire. They certainty weren't afraid to threaten murder against kidnapped victims that night. I guess the most profound statement came from Duco when he was released and interviewed by a reporter. The reporter asked Duco, "Looking back Duco, what would you have done differently?" Duco replied, "I would have killed the witnesses." My Dad asked him the same question and the reply was then same. I believe the gang was very capable of committing murder.

My best friend is a 27 year police officer. We discussed the topic of murder and if he thought they committed it or not. He said that he has been involved in many homicide investigations and interviewed many suspects, and his opinion is that these people were more than capable of committing the ultimate crime.

I talked with a psychologist about this scenario, he said the same thing. His professional opinion is that they were very capable of murder.

This of course is all speculation and suspicion. The questions were all asked in a hypothetical forum. I'm not accusing any of them of committing murder, I only hold suspicion. If there are in fact unsolved murders in southern Minnesota, northern Iowa or eastern South Dakota during the years of 1931 – 1933, perhaps this gang should be included in your investigations.

During the later parts of 1990 and early 1991, Mabel was always putting one foot in her grave. She constantly complained about one health issue or another. She always thought she was dying. More than once the nursing staff called everyone and said Mabel was close to death. We would all rush to her side only to discover that she was fine, false alarm.

On June 24, 1991 we all received a call from the home. They stressed it was for real this time. Mabel went into a coma and her breathing was labored. When I arrived she had a small come back. She was whispering to my mom. I later found out that my mom asked one more time who her real dad's name was. Mabel still refused to tell her. A few minutes later she went unconscious and a few seconds later exhaled her last breath. Her era was over. I didn't shed any tears; neither did anyone else in the room at the time. A few days later we conducted the funeral. The family attended and I didn't notice anyone that would resemble friends. A testimony on how she treated people.

My mother went through her life asking her mother, "Who is my father?" It was a question that was asked frequently. Mabel would always give an excuse not to tell her the name. Mabel knew who it was. Why wouldn't she tell his name? Mabel was a very busy prostitute. She had to be in order to earn money for rent and food. I don't care what his name is. I want to know why it's so important for Mabel to keep his name a secret. I'll probably never know unless I have my DNA compared to a national data DNA bank. The family may be traced that way, but at what cost? Maybe some day, but until that day comes or if it doesn't, I have jut one piece of advice for the majority of you, If Grandma's in Heaven, Watch Out!

ACKNOWLEDGMENTS

This book could never have been written if it weren't for a few people in my life that not only encouraged me, but through long discussions helped me formulate some of the opinions and conclusions. When a book is written about family members and their inclusion is needed to present to truth and consequences it takes special people to allow them to be exposed. So I dedicate this book to my family and friends who I love dearly and cherish their friendship always.

>A special thanks to my wife for supporting me through the whole process.

>Thanks to my aunt who has provided opinions and advice with a bit of prodding.

>Thanks to my best friend, the person who read the manuscript and cheered me on.

>I would like to thank The Minnesota Historical Society for allowing me to gather newspaper accounts of this family tragedy and there excellence in cataloging the information in such away, people like me can get to the information they need effortlessly.

A special thanks to the following list of people and organizations that have supplied me with hard copy information and interviews. As requested by some, there names have been omitted and there only titles listed.

1. Minnesota Department of Corrections
2. Benson Police Chief (Ret) and Montevideo Police Chief (Ret)
3. Guards and staff at the Stillwater State Prison
4. Minneapolis Star and Tribune
5. St. Paul Dispatch and Pioneer Press
6. Swift County Historical Society
7. Minnesota Bureau of Criminal Apprehension
8. Minnesota Board of Parole
9. Jennifer Leigh, Editor. Jen made this book readable.

Most of all, I would like to thank my mother Darlos who is now getting all the answers she needs. She passed away June 30, 2004 still not knowing who her real father was.

My mother talked with me for hours on end about her memories of the family tragedy back in 1933. Late night conversations over hot cocoa and tears brought out the worst in her mother, Mabel, and the best in my mother. I thank her for opening her heart to me. She wanted a book written about this experience, so she made every effort to tell me everything that happened through out all our lives.

I want to see my mother at peace for once. The look she had in the picture with the dress Mabel made in prison is the look my Mother carried her whole life. Nothing could compensate her or make her forget the horrors she endured as a child. Nothing could overcome the feelings that were raw from her mother calling her the unwanted one, the continued sexual abuse when she was a small child or withholding the information my mother desperately wanted. The cruelty I witnessed by Mabel makes my blood boil even today. That's why I say, "If Grandma's in Heaven, Watch Out!"

About the Author

To begin with, I'm not a true author. I'm a retired professional truck driver with a few years of being a Park Ranger tossed in rounding out my life experiences. The story I wrote is a true story about my felonious grandparents. I have researched everything in this book through various media including newspapers, historical societies, and interviews.

They were a seven member gang during the 1930's and were caught with a hail of bullets. Even though they are my grandparents and great uncles, I didn't pull any punches writing about them. They were cruel and extremely dangerous people. The truth has now been told. Once you have read this story, its title becomes very clear.

If Grandma's in Heaven, Watch Out!

For years I have kept a promise to my mother in keeping the knowledge of my grandmothers' participation secret. I promised my mother that when grandma passed away I would publish the dirt my grandmother rubbed my mothers' life in. Now that they are both gone and the word is out, I can be assured that my mother is finally vindicated and can now rest in the peace she so justly deserves.

There is nobody closer to the truth about the gangs' activities then me. This is their true story as I know it.

Ken Halverson